# The Doubting Disease

 *Integration Books*

STUDIES IN PASTORAL PSYCHOLOGY,
THEOLOGY, AND SPIRITUALITY
Robert J. Wicks, General Editor

also in the series

# The Doubting Disease

## *Help for Scrupulosity and Religious Compulsions*

Joseph W. Ciarrocchi

Integration Books

*paulist press/new york/mahwah*

*Cover design by Tim McKeen.*

The Target Symptoms List (Figure 6-2) and the Obsessions and Compulsions Checklist (Appendix B) are from the Yale-Brown Obsessive-Compulsive Scale and are used with permission of the Department of Psychiatry of Yale University School of Medicine.

Library of Congress Cataloging-in-Publication Data

Ciarrocchi, Joseph W.
    The doubting disease : help for scrupulosity and religious compulsions / Joseph W. Ciarrocchi.
        p.   cm. — (Integration books)
    Includes bibliographical reference and index.
    ISBN 0-8091-3553-1
    1. Scruples.   2. Obsessive-compulsive disorder.   3. Pastoral counseling.   I. Title.
II. Series
BV4012.2.C5178  1995                                            94-25222
253.5—dc20                                                          CIP

Published by Paulist Press
997 Macarthur Boulevard
Mahwah, NJ 07430

Printed and bound in the
United States of America

# Contents

To my children with all my love:
Michael, Laura, Katie, Jennifer, and Daniel.
May a thousand difficulties never equal a
single doubt.

# Acknowledgments

It must seem odd that in a world with too few scruples, one presumes to write about the affliction of their excess. Nevertheless, the plight of those who see sin where none exists has fascinated me for over twenty years. I feel driven to understand it, for I now believe that scrupulosity represents a model to understand broad and more serious issues relating to religion and mental health. The persons described in this book are the least aggressive and most gentle of any I know. Yet, I am convinced that the non-acceptance of our all-too-human impulses and feelings may lead some religious persons eventually to act out the forbidden. But that would be another book.

For the present book I need to express my appreciation to those who assisted me so generously. In particular, the Loyola College pastoral counseling community provided both material and spiritual support. Pam Wicklein typed transcripts and tracked down the bulk of the references. Sister Shirley Peace proofread the entire document, rounded up many elusive citations, and typed the figures and worksheets. My editor, Bob Wicks, encouraged me from the beginning and allowed me to use him as a motivational influence. The librarians for Loyola College in Maryland were infinitely patient and helpful, even when we lost citations they had painstakingly found earlier. I want to thank reference librarians Judith Osborn and Geraldine Hall, as well as Mary Beverungen, the librarian who coordinated the large number of interlibrary loans.

My son, Michael, insisted on rescuing me from premature obsolescence by tutoring me in the latest update of Word Perfect. He also provided the graphic layouts.

Two groups have most shaped this book. First, the dozens of persons with scrupulosity or obsessive-compulsive disorder who honored me by seeking my help over the past fifteen years. I have always felt drawn to them for reasons that are unclear even to me. Perhaps I simply hate seeing religious faith experienced as personal condemnation. They have taught me what I know about the problem, and have challenged me to create strategies that could be useful.

The second group is my classroom teachers of moral theology and philosophy of twenty-five years ago: Urban Adelman, Charles Curran, Ronald Lawler, Edmund Quinn, and Myles Schmitt. Priests all and gentlemen, each was passionate *and* civil in discourse. Their views helped me respect tradition and see that ancient principles could shed light on human behavior that moderns are finally recognizing as an emotional disorder.

# Foreword

*The Doubting Disease* by Joseph W. Ciarrocchi brings to the fore the most current information available today on religion and scruples, scrupulosity, and obsessive-compulsive disorders (OCD). In this book he helps us clearly appreciate the interior anguish suffered by thousands of people of faith who have this symptomatology and what we can do about it.

As an expert in OCD who has dual credentials in psychology and theology, he provides a balanced and insightful view into the (potentially positive and negative) roles religion can play in scrupulosity. In the process of doing this, he debunks some of the widely-accepted but unsupportable myths about the connection between faith and this type of pathology.

As well as offering a concise, helpful understanding of the demographics, etiology and treatment of scrupulosity and OCD, in *The Doubting Disease* he also addresses the questions:

- How does scrupulosity develop?
- What are the differences between common and uncommon scrupulosity?
- What are some classic and contemporary models of religious scrupulosity?
- Where does the issue of scrupulosity fit into the history of pastoral care?
- What are some practical ways to target scruples and increase motivation for reduction of scrupulosity and compulsivity?
- How and when should persons get help for scrupulosity and OCD?

In addition in his final chapter ("Technical Asides: Moral Reasoning, Scruples, and the Psychology of Religion"), he addresses the futility of

1

attempting to convince someone to give up scruples through argumentation and offers insight into what religion can learn in general from the psychology of scruples. And, for professional counselors interested in this topic, the appendices he provides also offer invaluable clinical guides for step-by-step treatment.

Essential for all persons involved in general ministry, pastoral counseling, and the treatment of religious persons suffering from scrupulosity and OCD, I believe this book will also be of great service for anyone interested in the psychology of religion and the theological topics of "conversion," "discernment," and "sin."

*The Doubting Disease: Help for Scrupulosity and Religious Compulsions* by Joseph W. Ciarrocchi then is a fine work of scholarship that is written in a compassionate, helpful fashion. It integrates psychology and religion and puts professional knowledge in an important area at the service of persons in pastoral care. And, given the topic, it is a work that has been long needed by counselors and ministers alike.

Robert J. Wicks
Series Editor

**Part One**

# SCRUPLES:
# ORIENTATION AND OVERVIEW

*Chapter 1*

# Scrupulosity: An Overview

### What Are Scruples and Scrupulosity?

Spiritual guides have long recognized how an overly sensitive moral conscience interferes with living a life based on faith. The term "scrupulosity" refers to seeing sin where there is none. Some call it a "phobia concerning sin."[1] The person judges personal behavior as immoral that one's faith community would see as blameless. The dictionary defines a scruple as an ethical objection that inhibits action.[2] The word itself comes from the Latin word *scrupulum* for small sharp stone. This word creates an image of walking with a stone in your shoe. Another meaning for the word in Latin is a small weight as a unit of measure equal to about 1.3 grams. A scrupulous person, therefore, is one who is very conscientious and exacting.[3]

The French label the emotional condition which is sometimes part of scrupulosity "the doubting disease." This describes well the dilemma of the scrupulous. They feel uncertain about religious experiences and do not find reassurance through the normal means available to them. Consider the following illustration:

> The Smith family traditionally joins hands around the dinner table to give thanks in prayer before the meal. Susie, age four, and Billy, age six, sometimes are fidgety (and always hungry). Mrs. Smith worries that Susie, Billy, and perhaps herself have not "truly prayed" due to the multiple distractions: Susie is scratching her mosquito bite, Billy is leering at the chocolate pudding, and Mrs. Smith remembers she has a school board meeting after dinner. She doubts that their prayers were "heard," and so requests that the family repeat their prayers. Sometimes she makes the whole family repeat them, and sometimes only the children.

Once the children needed to repeat them four times, even though Mr. Smith tried to intervene after the second time. Mrs. Smith has sought advice from her pastor who urged her not to repeat the prayers, either for herself or the children. When she attempts to follow this advice, however, her entire meal is ruined as she attempts to sort out in her head whether this is acceptable to God. She will continue to worry about it throughout the rest of the evening, including her school board meeting.

Most people will recognize the absurdity of Mrs. Smith's religious doubt as a legitimate "moral" problem. Most, however, will not have the capacity to appreciate the intensity or duration of worry she experiences over this seemingly trivial matter. Although problems of scrupulosity are a matter of degree, some will have their entire lives paralyzed as a result of such problems. Still more will suffer a mostly private anguish, sharing their fears with only a few trusted friends or spiritual advisors. Scrupulous persons recognize that their worries are not "normal" in the sense that other people share them. This leads to feelings of shame and efforts to hide their fears as much as possible.

The end result is that scrupulosity remains largely hidden from the religious community at large. Usually persons only approach religion professionals such as clergy. They believe they alone have such doubts, and this increases their shame and further isolates them from others. In helping such individuals I have often noticed the healing power of recognizing that one is not alone, and that others share the problem. For this reason hearing examples from history and clinical composites is often comforting.

### Conflicts with Mental Health Professionals

People with scrupulosity often face another dilemma. Frequently their religious worries are only one part of a larger problem with anxiety. Mrs. Smith, for example, might have other worries besides her prayer doubts. Perhaps she finds herself repeatedly checking the children in their beds at night to see if they are safe or have stopped breathing. This might disrupt the family so much (by waking up her husband and children) that she seeks professional help.

What happens next varies greatly. Sometimes the therapist is knowledgeable about this specific type of anxiety and will ask questions about related doubts including religious worries. A thorough assessment, therefore, usually uncovers scrupulosity. On occasion the therapist may not be familiar with the range of symptoms for Mrs. Smith's anxiety disorder. This disorder, which will be described in detail in Chapter 2, is called obsessive-compulsive disorder, and is quite complicated. Some therapists have much experience in treating it, but others have none. Those with little experience may not appreciate how the disorder intrudes into the religious domain. Therefore, they may not ask questions about this area of a person's life. Further, as mentioned above, the client may be embarrassed about scrupulosity or believe therapy is not the proper forum to discuss it. The client may also worry that in offering an honest description of his or her symptoms the professional will "think that I am crazy" or worse.

> Bob is a twenty-eight year old married Jewish man who works for an accounting firm. He is thrilled with the birth of his first child, a bubbly infant girl. Bob has vowed to be totally involved with her as a parent and share in all aspects of child-care. He was shocked by the following experience: Bob was changing his daughter's diaper when the thought, idea, or image (he wasn't quite sure which) flashed through his mind—"Touch her private parts." The first time it happened he shuddered, tried to dismiss the idea, and hurriedly completed diapering her. All day he tried not to think about it. The next time he changed her diaper, however, the idea came back, but this time in the form of a graphic picture of Bob engaging in the dreaded behavior. This time he felt nausea, became dizzy, and called his wife to finish, saying he thought he was ill and would pass out. The idea began to torment Bob. He found himself not wanting to be alone with his daughter, lest he "give in" to this impulse. He refused to bathe her or change her diaper. Sensing something was drastically wrong his wife urged him to seek help. He talked to his rabbi who tried to reassure him that he was not a child molester and should dismiss the thoughts. When Bob could not do this, the rabbi referred him to a psychiatrist. Therapy explored several possibilities. One was that Bob was ambivalent about child-care, that his symptoms represented an unconscious attempt to

escape being a "modern" father. This "secondary gain" allowed him to avoid distasteful aspects of child-care. He and his therapist also explored how "incestuous" feelings are commonplace. Still Bob was not comforted. He sought out a therapist in a community mental health clinic. When Bob revealed the depth and extent of his imagery, the counselor wondered whether he would have to make a formal report to the state's Department of Child Welfare. Bob never returned.

Some encounter therapists who do not value religion, or the person's personal religious beliefs. These therapists maintain that the religious belief itself represents "neurosis," and that clients will improve only if they abandon their "infantile" beliefs. Naturally such encounters make a person wary of further contacts with the mental health field. The tendency for a committed believer is to rely exclusively on the religious support system.

### Does Religion Cause Scruples?

A superficial view may lead an observer to conclude, as do some mental health professionals, that religion is the source of scrupulosity. After all, a scrupulous man obsesses about sinning if he feels attracted to a pretty woman only because he believes this constitutes "committing adultery in his heart."

The superficial view fails to distinguish between religion causing the disorder from religion as its background. Religion does not cause scrupulosity any more than teaching someone French history causes him to believe he is Napoleon. All human beings exist in some cultural context. They have a language, a particular world-view, rules about interpersonal relationships, and so on. Cultural backgrounds provide the scenery around which emotional problems create the drama. The unfortunate person who believes he is Napoleon could just as well believe he is Jesus, Buddha, or Peter the Great in another setting. Science would waste a lot of time searching the cultural context for the cause of the man's psychosis.

This does not mean that religion plays no role in the origin of emotional difficulties. (We will discuss this intricate relationship more fully in Chapter 9.) Briefly, religion may contribute when its content is presented in an overly harsh, punitive manner. Students of such presentations are likely to associate the content of the religious message with fear and anxiety. Once fear is learned the laws of human behavior relating to fear take over. In susceptible individuals these laws of learning may then trigger extreme anxiety around religious issues or themes.

The key phrase here is "susceptible individuals." We have only a slight understanding of what makes a person susceptible to anxiety disorders (or, indeed, any emotional problem). Why does one person in a religious instruction class develop scrupulosity but the other fifteen do not? Teaching children to wash their hands before eating is normative in middle-class America. Only a few children instructed in this manner will spend countless hours washing their hands until the skin rubs off. Similarly, we cannot yet explain why learning about moral choices will become an impossible dilemma for some, causing untold agony in decisions about right and wrong. We will discuss some hunches about these questions in Chapter 2.

### Are Scruples Psychological or Religious?

The answer to the heading is yes. Scrupulosity might be an exclusively religious or psychological problem in some cases. More often it is both. We will discuss occasions when the problem is a purely developmental one. A person may go through a phase of life when religious concerns are prominent and scrupulosity emerges. In these instances instruction from the religious community eventually resolves the doubts or questions. For others, scrupulosity is a life-long problem which ebbs and flows in intensity and represents a significant emotional problem.

For those social critics who worry about "the diseasing of America" or other countries, they may rest assured we are not promoting still another category of "diseases" with still more victims.[4] Rather, scrupulosity as a psychological disorder is well understood in the context of abnormal psychology. As we will describe later, even church ministers viewed it as a psychological rather than religious disorder. Nor are we discussing the profound worries that arise in resolving the meaning of human existence. Indeed, rather than being freed from such concerns, our view is that moderns should spend more time pondering existential issues and so avoid the "escape from freedom" which characterizes our time. Existential worries, far from being disabling, contribute to our highest cultural and artistic achievements.

A related concern is that an individual with scrupulous problems may feel that to get better he or she will have to abandon religious belief. Indeed, I have treated clients who have reached this conclusion and leave organized religion entirely, believing that they are more at peace. The purpose of this book, however, is not to direct people's lives, but rather to suggest that a measure of relief is possible. I would invite the reader to distinguish between faith as it gives meaning to existence, and the pathology of faith which is scrupulosity. I cannot dictate anyone's solution to the pain of scrupulosity. I can, however, share my experience in treatment which suggests that a person can maintain a deeply committed religious faith *and* shed the burden of scrupulosity.

## Do People with Scruples "Lose Their Minds"?

The cases of Mrs. Smith and Bob in this chapter may indicate the degree of irrationality seen in scrupulosity. Both persons viewed their ideas and behavior as senseless yet felt compelled to carry it out. The irrationality of the ideas often makes people feel that they "are going crazy." Yet they are not. "Crazy" is usually reserved for psychotic behavior—behavior which represents a gross distortion of reality. When individuals are psychotic they typically *believe* the distortions: e.g. that they actually are Napoleon or Jesus. Bob and Mrs. Smith are in a painful middle ground. They know the ideas are senseless, yet feel enormously controlled by them. No wonder that such an intense split leads to wondering if they are "losing their minds." Some ask if they are "schizophrenic," i.e. believing that they are two people—a Dr. Jekyll and Mr. Hyde (not the true definition of schizophrenia).

If losing our minds means developing psychosis, scrupulous persons clearly do not. However, we do not have to be psychotic to have immense pain. Scrupulous persons frequently are in tremendous emotional pain and in need of help. They need reassurance that they are not losing their minds. To avoid receiving the label "crazy" they do not talk about their symptoms. An understanding professional, whether in the pastoral care or mental health field, will provide a trusting atmosphere which will allow persons to unburden themselves honestly.

## Outline of the Book

The book has three parts. *Part One* is an orientation and overview of scruples, and this first chapter defined scruples, examined the personal ordeal of sufferers, and briefly identified some common questions about the condition. Chapter 2 discusses the relationship between scruples and its sister-condition, obsessive-compulsive disorder (OCD). This chapter provides a description of OCD, its frequency in the general population, current causal theories and treatment methods. Chapter 3 describes the various types of religious obsessions and compulsions we call scruples. We look in depth at one historical example from the religious literature (John Bunyan) as well as examples from clinical practice. Chapter 4 examines the history of scruples in pastoral care. Pastoral care refers to how professional theologians and those entrusted with religious care viewed the problem.

*Part Two* is devoted to applying change strategies for scruples based on current psychological models for treating OCD. It represents the heart of the book for those interested in change for themselves or in helping others change. Chapter 5 looks at identifying scruples and developing motivation to change. Too often clinicians describe powerful treatment methods, but neglect the crucial problem of motivating people to take on these inconvenient and sometimes fearful procedures. Chapters 6 and 7 apply behavioral change principles to obsessional scruples and compulsive scruples, respectively. Chapter 7 also discusses helping change scruples in agnostics and the unchurched, since these groups require a slightly different perspective in pastoral care. Although we divide the obsessions and compulsions for explanatory purposes, change requires dealing with them simultaneously. This requires using Part Two as an entire unit rather than in segments.

*Part Three* covers several topics related to the practice and theory of changing scruples. Because so many clients I have worked with have described negative experiences with the mental health profession, Chapter 8 details strategies for finding qualified mental health professionals and religious counselors for treating OCD and scruples. Also discussed are the medications qualified psychiatrists use to treat OCD, as well as self-help organizations. The last chapter looks at a number of technical matters for the reader interested in questions about the nature of moral reasoning, whether religion causes scruples, and, finally, how the scientific study of scrupulosity may benefit the integration of psychology and religion.

I have included what I hope will be a user-friendly innovation through the extended Appendix. Part Two describes the heart of the change strategies so that the reader can understand the rationale for change. The sheer amount of information, however, could easily cause the reader to lose sight of the forest for the trees. I have had similar experiences in reading otherwise excellent books oriented toward self-change. To prevent this problem, therefore, I have condensed the change strategies into a more manageable size by eliminating the narrative text and placing the overview in the Appendix. The reader will also find the figures and worksheets from Part Two reproduced there. The Appendix can serve, then, as a mini-manual for changing scruples. Reading Part Two is essential for the proper use of the Appendix.

## Is Professional Help Necessary?

I came across this warning in the very first sentence of a guide book for the treatment of scruples written 45 years ago. "If you are a person troubled with scruples, this book is not for you. Don't read more than this first paragraph."[5] The writer goes on to say that the scrupulous person needs a good confessor to obey blindly, not a book.

Although we may smile at the writer's paternalism, we can also commend his honest attempt at truth-in-advertising. He raises issues which books for the general public must face: what can be promised to the reader, and what is the potential benefit or harm in reading the book and implementing its strategies.

Over two decades of experience with self-help books suggest that self-directed change is possible. Some examples of this include self-help books in the area of drinking problems and fear reduction.[6] Self-directed change has also worked for OCD. However, in all cases the books or manuals were given to readers by a competent professional, even if the professional gave no other advice. In other words, the personal change plan was at least professionally monitored. Therefore, we cannot make promises that a reader will improve simply from using the strategies in this book. We do know, however, as we review in Chapter 2, that the strategies described form the heart of today's treatment of choice. We also know that persons with OCD can improve with a self-directed plan. On the one hand my own scrupulous concerns prohibit promising too much. At the same time, my concern for the pain of people with scrupulosity leads me to conclude that it is unethical to hide this information from potential consumers.

I also want to alert the reader to a problem *some* may have. Some persons with scruples react to hearing the scrupulous symptoms of others. They worry that these ideas may form the basis for new scruples. This fear of "contamination" is common, and can be worked through using the strategies described in this book. However, if you have serious concerns about this issue, you need to know that a variety of scrupulous ideas are discussed in some detail. If this is a major concern, working with a professional while reading the book is advised.

## The Writer and Religious Diversity

Anyone who dares attempt a work that purports to help a problem with religious dimensions is entering a potential mine field of his or her own making. I find addressing a psychological and religious issue which intertwines literally with all the world religions personally intimidating. Even a lifetime of devotion to the study of scruples would not provide sufficient expertise to appreciate its impact on even the major world religions. I am, therefore, attempting something more modest. I hope that I will provide a clear framework for understanding scruples and the religious dimensions of OCD. This will allow diverse groups to use the principles to solve problems that develop within the context of their own traditions. At the same time, the reader needs to know that I approach the subject as a Catholic, but my aim is to be as broadly ecumenical as possible, since this problem cuts across all faith groups. I have found fascinating historical allusions to scruples in moral theology and pastoral care (Chapter 4), and these insights may benefit the integration of psychology and religion in other religious traditions as well.

I hope that my presentation will alert both counselors who are religion professionals and the general mental health professional community to understand and incorporate psychological strategies for scruples. Psychologist Allen Bergin has studied the lack of importance given to clients' religious beliefs by many therapists.[7] He suggests that therapists need sensitizing to religious cultural issues in the same way that training is needed for racial and gender concerns. I believe that the experience of clients with scruples and secular therapists proves Bergin's point.

The work of behavior therapists in the field of OCD represents a positive model for working with religious symptoms. Taking a neutral stance toward the truth or falsity of religious belief itself, behaviorists take the person's symptoms (thoughts, feelings and behavior) very seriously. If the client wants to change the symptom, the behavior therapist honors the request. The therapist views the symptom as a problem in and of itself and not just a symbol of an underlying "real" issue. This stance has led behavior therapists to devise models which can help us understand scruples as one form of OCD, and which take symptoms seriously even if they have a "religious" content.[8]

# Chapter 2

# Scruples and Obsessive-Compulsive Disorder

## Overview of Obsessive-Compulsive Disorder

Although Chapter 9 will provide a more comprehensive picture of scruples, we can distinguish at least two types from the onset. The first type I call *developmental scrupulosity*. The word developmental implies a stage people pass through. However, scruples are not limited to any particular phase. *A newly emerging sense of conscience* characterizes developmental scruples. Sensitivity develops to moral or ethical issues and this contrasts with previous indifference.[1]

Two situations tend to trigger developmental scrupulosity. The first is adolescence. Some youngsters focus excessively on sin as part of their religious and social development. Religious instruction inspires them to give themselves totally to God. Intellectual development drives the idealism common to this age.

> John is a serious fifteen year old boy who is active at church in Sunday school and attends as many adult education meetings as he can. He has become particularly sensitive about social justice issues: hunger in the world, the disparity between rich and poor nations, unemployment in his country, etc. John's behavior is driving his otherwise placid family to distraction. He eats a minimum amount of food each day (using his allowance for food relief in Africa). What disturbs his parents the most, however, are his constant harangues to his seven year old sister and five year old brother whenever he notices they waste food. They refuse to eat when he does, and more than one meal has ended with one of the little ones running from the table crying. When the parents raised this problem with their pastor,

15

she replied that she wished all the teenagers in the congregation had John's social conscience.

Adolescent developmental scruples tend to disappear as the youngster receives both challenges and further guidance. They often are "only a phase" a teenager goes through, although they may indicate a rich inner life and sensitivity to ethical concerns.

The second type of developmental scruples occurs in adults initially as part of a broader conversion experience: a response to a deeper exploration of life's meaning, one's faith or place in the universe. Martin Luther is one example. Prior to Luther's dramatic challenge to church practices in his day, he was beset with multiple scruples. Biographers discuss his preoccupation with sin and never feeling forgiven by God. This manifested itself in scruples still seen today in religious counseling: he would make repeated sacramental confessions for the same offenses, or would hurry back immediately after an imagined sin.[2] Luther's own working through this problem may have helped him develop his central insight of justification before God through faith.

St. Ignatius Loyola, founder of the Jesuits, is another historical example. A Spanish nobleman and soldier, Ignatius was severely wounded in battle and while recuperating experienced a profound religious conversion. This awakening of religious consciousness promptly threw him into a battle with scruples. Later when he wrote his guide to the spiritual life, he used an example from this early experience. He describes someone seeing two pieces of straw crossed on the path, and imagines that stepping on them is blasphemy by insulting the cross of Christ.[3]

Both forms of developmental scruples differ from the next type since the person usually grows out of them. They respond either to self-reflection or advice.

*Emotional scrupulosity* is a different story. Although developmental scruples may generate intense emotional disturbance, they lack the staying power of this second, more enduring form. In this type, scrupulosity represents specific symptoms for the emotional disorder *obsessive-compulsive disorder* (OCD). In this chapter we present an overview of OCD to place scrupulosity in its wider perspective. This will explain patterns that often appear senseless or strange. In the past ten to fifteen years clinicians have learned much about OCD from a flurry of well-designed research.[4] We can take advantage of these newer findings about OCD to understand and treat scruples at both the religious and psychological level.

Clinicians have long recognized OCD as a serious mental health problem. A new awareness of its impact, however, resulted from recent surveys. What was once believed to be an extremely rare disorder, about one person per thousand, exists at a rate of nearly two adults per hundred. In the United States, for example, this represents about four million adults.[5] Prevention and early identification efforts have grown with awareness that one half of the cases develop in childhood or adolescence. To put this in perspective with other mental health problems, the disorder is more common than schizophrenia (one percent) and about half as common as depression.

*Definition of OCD.* The standard definition of OCD includes the presence of *either* obsessions or compulsions which significantly interfere with normal functioning. An *obsession* is a persistent idea, image or impulse that the person views as intrusive and senseless. Usually the person tries to get rid of it. A *compulsion* is a repetitive act that a person feels compelled to carry out. The act does not usually make sense to the person even though he or she feels required to do it.[6] A potentially confusing part of the definition is that compulsions can also be *internal* or mental, e.g. saying a prayer to oneself in response to a blasphemous idea.

Advances in diagnosis and classification suggest five common types of OCD. The first is *obsessional checking*. The person worries that an act was completed properly, and feels compelled to check and recheck the work. The person spends excessive time preparing for bed by repeatedly checking door locks, windows, water taps, turning off the stove, etc. The person returns several times to see if the car headlights are off, if the emergency brake is on, or if the car is in proper gear. When leaving the house, he or she returns several times to see if the iron is unplugged or the coffee maker turned off. On occasion most people will check an item once. What characterizes obsessional checking is repeated checking, or the urge to check minutes after the previous one.

*Obsessional cleaning* involves excessive cleaning of either one's body (e.g. multiple hand washing or showers on a daily basis), or objects in one's environment (scrubbing the floor for hours). The person who cleans this way usually has contamination worries about germs or objects that could harm someone (e.g. broken glass).

*Obsessional slowness* involves extraordinary precision in carrying out activities, such that the person takes an excessive amount of time for otherwise routine acts. One may spend forty minutes making a bed, constantly stepping back to see if both sides of the bedspread hang down equally. Another person spends a half-hour in front of the mirror combing his hair to get it "just right" (motivated by anxiety, not vanity). He may wait until March to open Christmas mail.

*Obsessional doubting-conscientiousness* refers to doubting that something was done properly. Here the person worries about both acts of commission and omission. She may worry that she "offended" a neighbor by her tone of voice in her greeting. Or, she might doubt that she failed to greet her, even though she does so routinely. A person passes someone on the street, then has the thought that he killed the person. Although patently absurd (the "murder" would take place at lunchtime on a crowded downtown street), he imagines how this could have happened and even returns to the scene of the crime to find the person for reassurance. Many scruples are of this variety, and the doubts often concern committing a sin.

*Obsessional ruminating* is the final type. Ruminating describes a process of turning over and over again in the mind an idea or image. Here the person experiences frequent intrusive thoughts of an unpleasant and even horrible nature. A mother may have vivid images of her children being murdered, a husband may visualize his spouse dying in an auto accident. Scruples often result from these obsessions, since the thoughts may have an unpleasant religious content. The ideas or images are blasphemous, or urge the person to do something immoral.[7]

*Demographics of OCD.* In the United States the National Institute of Mental Health sponsored the largest general population survey of mental disorders. The survey found 1.5 percent of the population met criteria for a current diagnosis of OCD, and 2.5 percent met criteria at some point in their lifetime. In this same general population survey women outnumbered men two-to-one with the problem. However, surveys of people seeking treatment for OCD suggest a nearly equal gender ratio. This may mean that severe forms of OCD are distributed equally between men and women.[8]

We know considerably less about the incidence of scrupulosity since no population surveys exist. Studies of Catholic students found 25 percent of high school students described scrupulous behavior and

14 percent of college students.[9] These are older studies, so we have less confidence in the percentages for young Catholics today.

Gender differences include age of onset and symptom subtypes. In adults the disorder appears earlier in men (average age 20) than in women (average age 25).[10] The same is true for children, with boys having an earlier average onset (10 years old) than girls (13 years old).

Family background studies find great variation in the number of first degree relatives who also have OCD.[11] The percentages range from less than 1 percent up to 21 percent. Although OCD runs in families with a greater frequency than the general population, no convincing evidence yet exists for a genetic basis, as is true for some forms of mental illness. Parents who have OCD or their spouses often worry about transmitting the problem to their children. The majority of children of parents who have OCD seem to function quite well.

People with OCD who seek treatment have higher average scores on intelligence tests than the general population. We do not know if this is true for those who do not seek treatment, but it confirms clinical experience that OCD clients have above-average intelligence.

OCD is somewhat unusual for adult mental disorders in that its exact form may begin in childhood. Advances in classification can confirm the diagnosis at an early age, which should aid prevention efforts. OCD symptoms in childhood resemble OCD in most cases two to seven years later. As many as two-thirds of children diagnosed with OCD have the condition later. As some have remarked, the condition "breeds true" over time. This, again, highlights the importance of early diagnosis and treatment.

Anxiety disorders generally manifest themselves in young adulthood, and OCD follows this pattern. Most cases have appeared by age 30, and first episodes after age 50 are uncommon. About thirty percent of cases are evident by age 15. A large survey of high school students suggests that rates of OCD are about the same in adolescence as in adults (1.9%).[12]

People with OCD often have other mental health problems as well. Health specialists call this "co-morbidity." The following represents some estimates of co-existing problems for people with OCD: depression (31%); other phobias (46%); alcohol abuse (24%); other substance abuse (17%); panic disorder (13%). These high rates of other problems should alert counselors to the possibility of their masking OCD and scruples.[13]

## Description of OCD

We classify OCD as an anxiety disorder. Anxiety and fear play a normal and functional role in human life. Fear is adaptive, helping us to fight or flee danger. Anxiety or worry is also adaptive. In a poetic phrase, psychologist Howard Liddell termed it "the shadow of intelligence."[14] He saw anxiety as the price we pay for our ability to think about the future and make plans to improve our lives or avoid future catastrophes. The emerging concern for preventing environmental hazards to our planet is an example of adaptive worry. Few of our sister crickets or brother gorillas worry about ozone depletion.

For some people these "hard-wired" anxiety or fear reactions cross the boundary from functional to dysfunctional. Lower animals have instincts to avoid certain dangerous situations. For example, some small species avoid open spaces, since they are defenseless. The same behavior in humans becomes fear of shopping malls or other wide open areas (agoraphobia). For others, constant worry interferes with the ability to concentrate, complete tasks, or simply enjoy life. These worriers focus on problems common to all of us such as finances, family matters, health issues and so on. They are unable, however, to "let go" of their concerns. They may have trouble sleeping or else look tense and nervous. [15]

OCD seems to incorporate both these aspects of excessive anxiety, having the worst of both worlds. To an observer fear seems apparent. Many with OCD seem genuinely afraid of an object or situation (e.g. germs). At the same time worry is a key ingredient. They worry about health and safety issues or avoiding vague future catastrophes. In fact many describe the unpleasantness of OCD more like disgust or revulsion than fear.

Some experts, therefore, see *doubt* rather than anxiety as the core ingredient in OCD. Dr. Judith Rapoport of the National Institute of Mental Health (USA) describes OCD as people losing their ability "to know if they know something." [16] As we shall discuss, this inability to "truly know" plagues people with scruples. Nevertheless, OCD remains classified under anxiety disorders and is likely to remain so.

*OCD Symptoms.* The symptoms of OCD usually have two parts: obsessions and compulsions. We will describe each in detail. Most sufferers have both (80%), although one or the other may predominate in causing the person's distress.

Obsessions, as we have described earlier, involve ideas, images, urges, acts, situations or events which trigger anxiety. The person experiences them as unwanted and senseless. Many have attempted to classify obsessions and compulsions, and we will only highlight the more common ones. These categories are quite general and do not do justice to the infinite variety of obsessions (and compulsions) seen clinically.[17] We will use one study of 200 patients to illustrate the content and percentage of patients with an obsession.[18]

*Contamination* obsessions (45%) include the idea that the person has exposed himself/herself or others to dangerous germs or chemicals. One patient, who worked as a custodian in a school, refused to open storage closets for fear that the cleaning fluids would get on him and he would spread it to the children. A chemistry teacher would not send her pantsuit to the dry cleaners for fear that sulfuric acid was on it, and thus would harm the workers. Scruples are woven into contamination obsessions when the person worries that sin is involved because she did not take proper precautions. For example, if the chemistry teacher sends her suit to the cleaner, she may now obsess that in some way she is guilty of having exposed another to injury and needs forgiveness.

*Pathologic doubt* (42%) occurs when the person cannot feel certain that even the most elementary tasks were completed. Did I turn off my car lights? Is the stamp on this envelope precisely in the upper right hand corner so that the post office will accept it? Did I turn off the stove before leaving the house? What characterizes this obsession as different from normal worry or forgetfulness is that even after checking the doubt returns. Driving on an interstate highway at night, a car hits a mild bump in the road. The thought enters, "Did I run over someone?" In the area of religion, the person doubts that religious acts were performed properly. Were my prayers "acceptable" to God? When I saw that attractive person did I "lust in my heart"? A priest may obsess whether or not he validly performed the liturgical function, and whether or not it should be repeated.

*Somatic* obsessions (36%) refer to preoccupation with physical health in self or others. The person is hypervigilant to signs of illness and requires reassurance from medical authorities.[19]

*Need for symmetry* (31%). The person is excessively concerned with order and regularity regarding the positioning of objects. This is far beyond the personality trait of a concern for neatness and orderliness. With OCD the person experiences intense anxiety when items are not symmetrical or arranged precisely. Pencils must be lined up in a north-south direction on the desk; biographies cannot be interspersed with novels on the book shelf. The person spends endless time proceeding in a certain order. Numbers may have a controlling influence.

*Aggressive* obsessions (28%). These represent ideas, urges, or images around themes of hurting others. A woman describes her twenty-eight year old husband who will drive no faster than fifteen miles per hour in their city, no matter what the traffic conditions. A mother is terrified of hurting her newborn. She keeps the baby away from the sink (images of running scalding water over him), will not cover him with a blanket (fear of strangling him), and removes all heavy objects from sight, e.g. irons, frying pans (fear of hitting him over the head).[20]

*Sexual* obsessions (26%) are unwanted, persistent ideas, images or urges with a sexual theme. A happily married woman has constant graphic sexual images about a neighbor. A parent has persistent thoughts about touching his child's private parts while bathing her. A mother is bombarded with the idea that she is a lesbian and will "pass it on" to her children. A spouse complains to her husband's therapist that all their telephones have pillows tightly wrapped around them. The husband admits this is to prevent him from carrying out the urge to make obscene phone calls. Naturally, these images represent a fertile field for scruples. Many religious persons have clear standards about sexual behavior, and sexual obsessions usually are outside acceptable boundaries. Many will speak to a religious leader for reassurance that they have not sinned.

As indicated, several obsessional types provide the content for scrupulosity. Relevant ones include, but are not limited to, blasphemy, violence, psychological harm, and sexual obsessions.

The disturbing nature of obsessions and their persistence lead to the second major characteristic of OCD—that is, the need to resist these ideas and urges which result in *compulsions*. Although cases of OCD exist with only obsessions or compulsions, usually the two go together. Compulsions are repetitive acts that the person performs, yet knows are either senseless or out of proportion to the situation. As in the case of obsessions, compulsions, too, have different categories. The following represent the more common types.[21]

*Checking* compulsions (63%) represent the person's quest for certainty regarding the obsessive doubts. The driver who went over the bump in the road drives five miles to the next exit, turns around and searches the fields with a flashlight for an hour looking for the body. He even may report the "accident" to the state police. A driver takes ten minutes to back his car out of the driveway, repeatedly checking his rear-view mirror for children playing, and even getting out of the car two or three times to check. People with safety obsessions (leaving appliances plugged in, doors unlocked) will spend minutes or even hours repeatedly checking these items. Since the doubt reoccurs even after checking, the checking never seems to end.

*Washing* compulsions (50%) relate to contamination obsessions and the desire to eliminate germs or other contaminants. Checking and washing compulsions represent the two most frequently seen compulsions in clinical practice. Some wash their hands or other body parts so frequently they develop skin disorders. Some take multiple showers. For others the washing becomes a ritual after certain acts or thoughts. A person who masturbates in his bed develops a ritual of showering and washing all sheets, pillow cases, blankets and bed covers. In literature, of course, we have the famous example of Lady Macbeth who spends her nights washing her hands in guilt for participation in the king's murder. "What, will these hands ne'er be clean?" (*Macbeth*, Act V, Scene 1) could well be the slogan for this set of compulsions.

*Counting* compulsions (36%) are the counterpart to need-for-symmetry obsessions. Those with a need for symmetry feel compelled to count acts or objects so that they are "correct." Mary needed to touch her face after washing precisely six times, and if something interfered, she would need to start over and complete the six touches.

The compulsion *to ask or confess* (31%) underlies obsessions that one has caused physical or other harm to someone. A mother who mildly brushes up against her child asks ten times for reassurance that she did not injure the child. A spouse believes a certain look on his wife's face meant he hurt her feelings and thirty minutes of reassurance do not remove the doubt. People with OCD are well known to police for "confessing" to sensational crimes that they did not commit. Several years ago a serial child murderer stalked Atlanta, Georgia. Three OCD clients "confessed" to me that they killed the children. Despite living nearly a thousand miles away, one insisted she woke up in the middle of the night in an hypnotic state, flew to Atlanta, committed the murder, flew back, and never woke up her sleeping spouse before his six o'clock rising time.

*Symmetry and precision* compulsions (28%) are the counterpart to the need-for-symmetry obsessions. One patient selected his recreational reading material in bookstores by going through the Dewey Decimal

Classification in sequence. For example, if he read a book last month in the 200 section (philosophy), this month he would have to select one from the 300 section (social sciences), and so on with each successive book. Some will count the strokes while brushing their teeth, or feel obligated to tap an object an exact number of times before using.

*Hoarding* compulsions (18%) go considerably beyond the "pack-rat" personality trait of many who like to collect objects or artifacts. Some "collect" newspapers, not for any real purpose, but feel intense anxiety if they are thrown out. Someone else never throws out mail including "junk" mail. One person has dozens of boxes with food coupons that take up all available apartment space, and spends hours cataloging them even though many are outdated. Hoarding compulsions seem fueled by the obsession that "someday I might need these things." Family members report that when they get fed up and finally "clean house," the person with OCD watches with a look of genuine terror. To minimize the distress, many clean up only when the person is not present. Behavior which looks like laziness or contentment with squalor may actually mask an OCD hoarding compulsion.

One can see how compulsions easily enter the religious domain. People pray in response to blasphemous images; they seek endless reassurance from people they "injure"; they repeat religious rituals not performed "properly"; and they constantly ask spiritual guides for reassurance about the state of their soul.

## Psychological Origins of OCD

The words obsession and compulsion have a variety of meanings in everyday conversation. We have perfumes that are named for each, and several movies appear annually with "obsessed" lovers who murder their rejecting love object. In this section we will examine possible psychological origins for OCD, and see its relation to normal obsessions. We will also examine how OCD differs from the use of similar terms in daily conversation.

*OCD Versus Normal Obsessions.* Distinguishing normal obsessions from OCD thinking gives a clearer perspective to the dysfunctional nature of OCD. Most people experience odd, eccentric or horrifying images or urges. This, no doubt, comes from our mind's capacity to imagine both real and contrived events. The good self-observer may notice that these images often arise when we are tired or feeling low.

Most of us can dismiss these obsessions without difficulty, or at least distract ourselves.

In a study of people without OCD, nearly 80 percent reported experiencing obsessions at some time.[22] Trained clinicians had difficulty distinguishing these obsessions by content from those reported by persons with OCD. People without OCD differed in that their obsessions were less frequent, were easier to dismiss, were less upsetting, and more acceptable. People with OCD also felt a greater urge to neutralize the obsessions. Obsessions, therefore, are part of normal experience. They appear to be less frequent, less disturbing, and have less staying power than in OCD.

Of course the intriguing question is: *Why* do obsessions differ in OCD from others?[23] Two separate mechanisms may be at work here, although we know little about the ultimate causes of OCD, or indeed most emotional problems. The first is suggested by psychologist David Barlow.[24] He believes people with OCD may be predisposed to develop an anxiety disorder by first possessing a high degree of "nervous" energy. That is, their bodies react to events with greater levels of anxiety than others, and this tendency exists from an early age. But, people with OCD require another dimension. Barlow suggests that what separates OCD from other anxiety disorders is that people come to believe that *certain kinds of thoughts are dangerous in themselves.*[25] In other words, if I think certain thoughts either the events will happen, or I truly am the kind of person who would actually do such things. Every parent observes a version of this thinking process in their 2-4 year old children. The child believes that if he can imagine the existence of wild creatures in his closet, surely they must exist.

Scrupulosity fits this picture perfectly. People with scruples believe, "If I have this thought, image or impulse, *I must be that kind of person or be willing to do those things.*" The person then focuses on religious statements about the importance of a "clean" mind or a "pure spirit." Further, God knows what is in our hearts.

But all people of faith hear essentially the same messages. Why do only a few respond with scrupulosity, and why do only some people in society develop OCD? Perhaps a second mechanism is also at work for these individuals. Social psychologist Daniel Wegner suggests this may relate to faulty methods of mental control.[26]

In a clever series of experiments people were first asked to think aloud for five minutes about anything that came to mind. Then one group was asked *not* to think about white bears. On average, persons told not to, mentioned white bears six times over the next five minutes. We have a difficult time suppressing our thoughts through sheer will power. But that was not all. Then the participants were asked to think aloud again for five minutes, and try to think about white bears as often as possible. On average they thought about white bears significantly more after trying to suppress the thought (16 times), than people told at the outset to think about them (12 times). *Thoughts actually accelerate after we try to suppress them.*

Now we can see how the stage is set for scruples and OCD. First, the person believes that certain thoughts are dangerous. Unacceptable thoughts, images or urges then trigger considerable anxiety. Anxiety forces a person to get rid of the thought. Now the "white bear" phenomenon kicks in, so that the more the person tries to suppress the thought the more frequent and intense it becomes. Since the thought is unacceptable, the person cannot just let it be. The person searches for a way to "neutralize" it. If the thought is about injury or harm, seek reassurance. If it involves worry about germs or contamination, take corrective action. The corrective action relieves the anxiety (temporarily), and, in the language of learning theory, reinforces the corrective action. What is reinforcing tends to get repeated, and the OCD\scruples cycle is thus born.[27] Figure 2-1 represents a model for the development of scrupulosity based on theoretical descriptions of Barlow and Wegner.

## OCD and Related Terms

We use the terms obsession and compulsion in a precise way for OCD. Everyday language has other meanings and we should distinguish them to avoid confusion. In conversation, people often discuss their "obsessions." They may mean food, alcohol, drugs, or a new sports car. These obsessions differ from OCD in that the items are enjoyable or pleasant in themselves.[28] They do not trigger the degree of disgust and revulsion that OCD obsessions do. This feature also separates OCD from addictions. Members of Alcoholics Anonymous sometimes describe alcoholism as an obsessive-compulsive disease. This is true in the sense that thoughts about drinking are obsessive, and one feels compelled to drink. However, drinking in and of itself is a pleasurable activity (if not, why pursue it?). The recovering alcoholic does not want to have alcohol on his or her mind, so the thoughts become intrusive during the recovery phase. But in OCD the obsessions themselves, at any stage, are repulsive and unpleasant. The compulsion for the alcoholic is to drink, not to neutralize the obsession as in OCD. In an addiction the compulsion enacts the obsession; in OCD the compulsion counters the obsession.

*Worries* also differ from obsessional thinking in both content and style.[29] Worries are usually related to the stuff of ordinary life. Financial problems, family troubles, occupational difficulties, and health concerns are the top four worry themes. Although persistent and anxiety provoking, they are not alien to the person as are obsessions. We do not experience worry themes as disgusting and repulsive as we do with obsessions. Indeed, we sometimes have trouble letting go of these worries precisely because we seem to want to keep mulling them over and over. Worry is what keeps us awake at night or impairs our concentration at other times. What makes extended worrying dysfunctional is that we merely "spin our wheels" rather than problem-solve. One worrisome idea simply leads to another in an endless chain, and we actually fail to solve a single issue. The result is a continual state of anxiety unless we distract ourselves or solve the problem.

*Depression* can both trigger obsessional thinking in itself as well as aggravate OCD. As noted above, most people are prone to obsessional thinking when they feel sad or blue. We feel we have not lived the right kind of life, we lock in on the dumb job decision we made ten years ago, or we regret past misdeeds. People with clinical depression often have the same patterns of obsessional thinking as in OCD. They differ from OCD in that they end when the person's mood improves, and usually there is no great urge to neutralize the obsession through a ritual. Indeed, depressed persons have a morbid fascination with the obsession and dwell on it endlessly.

On the flip side of the coin, depression occurs often in OCD. Some studies have found that up to 80 percent of people seeking treatment for OCD have had significant depression. People with OCD and depression sometimes improve on both dimensions with proper treatment.

*OCD and obsessive-compulsive personality.* We all know persons with an obsessive-compulsive personality. We may be one ourselves. OCD as a disorder differs from the personality trait. People with the personality trait prefer an orderly, organized life. They tend to work hard and may appear slightly uptight to their more relaxed peers. People with OCD, as you may have gathered from the examples under obsessions and compulsions, have narrow areas of concern. One germ-phobic

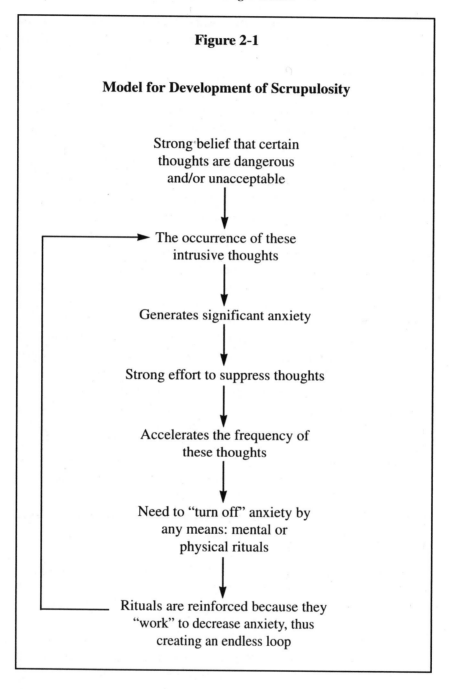

**Figure 2-1**

**Model for Development of Scrupulosity**

Strong belief that certain
thoughts are dangerous
and/or unacceptable

The occurrence of these
intrusive thoughts

Generates significant anxiety

Strong effort to suppress thoughts

Accelerates the frequency of
these thoughts

Need to "turn off" anxiety by
any means: mental or
physical rituals

Rituals are reinforced because they
"work" to decrease anxiety, thus
creating an endless loop

woman had two bathrooms in her apartment. Because she feared the disinfectants needed to clean, she neglected one bathroom to the point that it grew mold over all surfaces and became unusable. Gradually the same thing happened to the second bathroom as well, and she had to use the public lavatory in a building across the street. The clutter resulting from a hoarding ritual is another situation that an obsessive-compulsive personality could not tolerate. Some with OCD have contradictory ethical behavior which is less likely in an obsessive-compulsive personality. One man had elaborate cleansing rituals after masturbation at home but frequented sexually-oriented massage parlors and houses of prostitution with no sense of guilt.

Although every human being "has" a personality, for some their personality style is inflexible and maladaptive, causing personal distress for the individual or major interpersonal problems. We label these exaggerated personality styles as *personality disorders.*[30] Some people may have an exaggerated obsessive-compulsive personality style which is a true disorder. A person with this disorder may "play by the rules" in minor matters and harm the mission of the organization, or be so dedicated to work that he or she neglects other important life areas ("workaholism"). Although, in theory, someone with OCD might also have this personality disorder, we do not see this commonly in clinical practice. The unfortunate use of the same terms for two rather different conditions serves to confuse the lay public and mental health community alike.[31]

### Treatment

*Biological Influences and Treatment.* The cause or causes of OCD are unknown. Biological theories rely on several sources.[32] Brain studies that measure active or inactive areas of the brain have noted that OCD patients tend to have slower metabolism in the frontal area. Second, medications that help OCD work on a specific chemical messenger (serotonin) in the nervous system. Third, animal studies examining damaged brain areas notice OCD-like behavior from certain injuries. For example, if certain brain areas are removed, a nesting bird continues to build her nest without stopping. This suggests a missing "switch" in the brain that tells the bird to stop repeating the behavior. Some have speculated that this resembles continuous checking in OCD.

Although these reports are promising, we cannot conclude that biological sources are the cause of OCD. Current methods of investigation cannot tell us if biological changes are the cause or the effect of OCD. When two events are related, A may cause B, B may cause A, or C may cause both A and B. The traditional example in introductory research courses is the relationship between crime and the number of places of worship. Crime in any given area increases in direct proportion to the number of churches. Therefore, can one conclude that religion causes crime? As a moment's thought reveals, both are related to a third ingredient—increase in population.[33]

Even though serotonin is implicated by the drug studies, some studies find that the treatment medications increase the level, but others find that serotonin decreases.[34] Nor should we forget that brain activity also changes through environmental forces. Chemical messengers in the brains of infant monkeys change notably when they are separated from their mothers. OCD may change biological processes through the environmental changes associated with the behavior.

Nevertheless, medication is an effective treatment for many with OCD. The group of medications that are most helpful for OCD belong to a class of medications known as the antidepressants. Originally developed to treat depression, some have had good results with OCD. Three relatively new compounds include clomipramine (Anafranil), fluoxetine (Prozac), and sertraline (Zoloft). These medications are discussed in more detail in Chapter 8.

*Psychological Treatment.* Psychological theories about the causes of OCD remain unproven as well. We discussed the relevant theories of Barlow and Wegner above. Psychological treatment, however, already has an excellent track record in the form of behavior therapy.

Behavior therapists noticed the similarity between OCD and phobic behavior. Because behavioral strategies were so effective with phobias, the same strategies were employed. Behavioral treatment for phobia involves some form of exposure to the feared object or event, usually through a gradual process (desensitization). The procedure, however, had limited success. Then in the late 1960s Aubrey Lewis in England devised a new strategy. In addition to exposing an OCD patient to a feared object (e.g. "contaminated" kitchen appliances), Lewis also prevented the person from engaging in the ritual (e.g. hand washing). Patients who stopped using their rituals obtained more complete relief and more rapidly than by other methods. These two components were called exposure and blocking (or, response prevention).[35]

Behavior therapists are committed to a scientific model, and they began studying the effectiveness of this model in great detail. Many studies indicated that the treatment provides relief for about 75 percent of those studied.[36] Research has found that it is equally effective as anti-depressant treatment, and some found that medication does not add anything to behavioral treatment alone.[37] In some cases combining behavior therapy and medication may help, but no group study has confirmed this as yet. Some people are inclined to medication, while others are opposed to medication either on principle or because of its various side-effects. We are fortunate to have two varied treatment approaches for this disorder.

## Conclusion

This description of OCD should clarify its intimate connection with scruples. Most often scruples will represent part of a cluster of OCD symptoms. Sometimes they will represent the total sum of OCD symptoms. Those with a chronic history of scrupulous behavior need evaluation by a competent mental health professional to ensure that all dimensions are addressed. The person will not improve much if he or she works on not repeating prayers with a religious counselor, yet stays up three hours at night checking door locks. We have spent considerable space distinguishing obsessions from compulsions. Each functions differently and each requires a different treatment strategy as we will discuss in Chapters 4-6. Next, we turn our attention to the religious dimensions of OCD known as scruples.

---

# Chapter 3

# Scruples: Common and Uncommon

In this chapter we will explore obsessions and compulsions in their religious manifestations. Historically they are called scruples. Throughout this book we are mainly concerned with debilitating scruples that occur in the context of obsessive-compulsive disorder (OCD). However, distinguishing developmental scruples from OCD scruples is difficult without knowing the person's history. Furthermore, the strategies we suggest in Part Two for self-care are useful for either type. To my knowledge, no study exists which indicates differences in the pattern of scruples between developmental and OCD scruples.

In the next chapter we explore the long spiritual and theological tradition in the history of treating scruples as a pastoral concern for religious persons. As expected, the language and descriptions for the religious tradition differ from clinical language. The religious tradition uses the term scruples in a generic sense to describe all phenomena associated with the problem. Clinicians, as we reviewed in the last chapter, distinguish two components: obsessions and compulsions. Since this clinical distinction will be useful when we turn to care and treatment of scruples, we will use this classification in describing scruples. Once again, obsessions are defined as ideas, images or acts which trigger anxiety. Compulsions are repeated acts, images or ideas which relieve anxiety (usually in response to obsessions).

## An Historical Example: John Bunyan

The Christian spiritual master, John Bunyan (1628-88), provides us with a vivid example of scruples.[1] Not only was he one of the most important religious and literary figures of his time, but he wrote a dramatic record of his ordeal. The record demonstrates that scruples have existed for centuries, and that some sufferers eventually find relief. One of his works, *Pilgrim's Progress*, is an allegorical tale of life's religious journey and is considered a classic in English literature.

His scruples, however, are best described in his autobiographical work *Grace Abounding*. His story is instructive in that he describes the classic features of scruples in a religious rather than psychiatric tradition.[2]

Bunyan notes that his concerns and sensitivity to moral transgressions began at an early age. As we observed in the previous chapter, obsessions and compulsions may first become evident in childhood. A second feature common to scruples, which I have observed clinically as well, is that scruples sometimes occur in persons who violate religious or moral rules without concern for some period in their lives.

> ...[as] a child, that I had few equals (especially considering my years, which were tender, being but few) both for cursing, swearing, lying, and blaspheming the holy name of God. (p.18)

Although we may smile today at Bunyan's degree of self-recrimination for boyhood foul language, his focus is interesting because these same transgressions will form the major content of his future adult obsessions. His obsessions will center mainly around blasphemous ideas. This suggests that his obsessions in adulthood were not totally random, but that the ideas and images which later assaulted him had free play around age nine or ten.

His capacity for obsessional thinking and rumination is evident early. Around this same time he reports terrifying nightmares.

> For often, after I have spent this and the other day in sin, I have in my bed been greatly afflicted, while asleep, with the apprehensions of devils and wicked spirits, who still, as I then thought, laboured to draw me away with them, of which I could never be rid. (p.19)

He also describes depression as the frequent, unfortunate by-product of obsession as we saw in the previous chapter.

> These things, I say, when I was but a child, but nine or ten years old, did so distress my soul, that then in the midst of my many sports and childish vanities, amidst my vain com-

panions, I was often much cast down, and afflicted in my
mind therewith, yet could I not let go my sins.... (p.19)

He next describes his adolescence and young adulthood as "...the
very ringleader of all the youth that kept me company, in all manner of
vice and ungodliness." (p.20) He observes perceptively that his nightmares ended at this same time, "...for my pleasures did quickly cut off
remembrance of them, as if they had never been." (p.19)

A number of people with scruples describe their late adolescence
and early young adulthood as relatively free from scruples. Some even
describe the period as one of almost indifference to select moral or
religious rules. We may speculate that the energy and exuberance of
adolescence instigate the person to behave impulsively, thus "flood-
ing" moral conscience. Repeated transgression eliminates the anxiety
formerly associated with rule violations. Then, with calm and control
returning in adulthood, intrusive thinking becomes problematic again
or for the first time.

Like St. Augustine and other famous religious converts, Bunyan
goes through a prelude to his conversion. He describes this as feeling
the necessity to change, yet feeling stuck in his current ways. He
describes using a Pascal's-wager-type twist to the moral realm to justify
his behavior. Since, he told himself, it was probably too late to reform,
and if he was going to be miserable in his damnation then, "...if I must
be so, I had as good be damned for many sins, as be damned for few."
(p.26) He then starts contemplating what would be the "sweetest" sins.

Bunyan also describes obsessions that are not religious in nature. As
we described in Chapter 2, safety and fear of injury are common obsessions. Listen to how Bunyan obsesses over fear of church bells in the
steeple-house falling on him.

> ...I began to think, *how if one of the bells should fall?* Then
> I chose to stand under a main beam, that lay overthwart the
> steeple, from side to side, thinking here I might stand sure;
> but then I should think again, should the bell fall with a
> swing, it might first hit the wall, and then, rebounding upon
> me, might kill me for all this beam; this made me stand in
> the steeple-door; and now, thought I, I am safe enough; for
> if the bell should now fall, I can slip out behind these thick
> walls, and so be preserved notwithstanding. [italics in the
> original] (p.31)

But even standing in a safe place under the steeple fails to reassure him. "...but then it came into my head, how if the steeple itself should fall?" And this thought:

> ...did continually so shake my mind, that I durst not stand at the steeple-door any longer, but was forced to flee, for fear the steeple should fall upon my head. (p.31)

This represents a classic description of obsessions ("the bells might fall on me"), in conjunction with compulsions (finding a safe place to stand).

The next phase of Bunyan's life describes a recurring pattern following his conversion. The pattern involved an intense experience of God's grace followed shortly by tormenting doubts about his personal salvation. The periods of doubt lasted anywhere from a few months to several years. He experienced grace as ecstasy; the doubt as an unending search for assurance of salvation. The doubt haunted him day and night, during which he felt totally condemned.

In the doubting phases his mind generated an ingenious variety of obsessions to plague him about the state of his soul. Those familiar with the history of Christianity will recall Martin Luther's similar worries about personal salvation, and how he solved these doubts through his belief in justification by faith alone.[3] (Bunyan later cites Luther's *Sermons* as being the most important book for his spiritual development next to the Bible.) Bunyan, however, took Luther's doubt one step further: *"But how can you tell if you have faith?"* (p.38, italics in original). To solve this he was tempted by what he recognizes as a "delusion."

> *That there was no way for me to know if I had faith, but by trying to work some miracle.* (p.39, italics in original)

Another doubt revolved around the idea, *"But how if the day of grace should be past and gone?"* (p.45, italics in original) In other words, salvation is theoretically possible, but I missed the boat. On another occasion he found himself "...fearing I was not called" (i.e. to salvation, p.48).

Bunyan followed the same pattern in each case. He would search scripture for some answer to his doubt. Each time he eventually found a quote which is the occasion for the grace or reassurance. The reassurance is usually brief. "But, alas! Within less than forty days I began to question all again." (p.58)

Some of the doubts arise from common-sense questions which any thoughtful believer might have. For example, the existence of other religions became a source of doubt.

> *How can you tell but that the* Turks *had as good scriptures to prove their* Mahomet *the Saviour, as we have to prove our Jesus is? And could I think, that so many ten thousands, in so many countries and kingdoms, should be without the knowledge of the right way to heaven (if there were indeed a heaven); and that we only who live in a corner of the earth, should alone be blessed therewith?* (p.60, italics in original[4])

*Blasphemous Obsessions.* Eventually these concerns about salvation itself give way to a more disturbing set of obsessions: blasphemous thoughts. The thoughts took various forms:

> I often found my mind suddenly put upon it to curse and swear, or to speak some grievous thing against God, or Christ His Son, of the Scriptures. (p.62)

Perhaps the most insidious of all Bunyan's scruples is the obsession that he had committed what Christian scripture calls "the unpardonable sin," the sin against the Holy Ghost. In its original version (Matthew 12:31-32), Jesus does not specify what the sin actually is.[5] This torment, by Bunyan's account, lasted two-and-a-half years. Not only did he wonder whether he may have committed the sin, he also experienced, as is the case with OCD obsessions, *the urge to commit the sin.* He describes the power of this impulse:

> In these days, when I have heard others talk of what was the sin against the Holy Ghost, then would the tempter so provoke me to desire to sin that sin, that I was as if I could not, must not, neither should be quiet until I had committed it; now no sin would serve but that. (p.63)

As described in Chapter 2, a key aspect of obsessional thoughts is that the person resists them strenuously. Bunyan, despite all his doubts and sense of personal vileness, knew within himself that the obsessions were contrary to his value system.[6] He describes this resistance eloquently:

> Only by the distaste that they gave unto my spirit, *I felt there was something in me that refused to embrace them.* (p.61, italics in original)

This inner resistance manifests itself outwardly in behavior intended to counteract the obsessions. We now know that this neutralizing behavior evolves into compulsions. Bunyan describes a variety of compulsions.

> ...and in so strong a measure was this temptation [to commit the sin against the Holy Ghost], that often I have been ready to clap my hand under my chin, to hold my mouth from opening; and to that end also, I have had thoughts at other times to leap with my head downward into some muckhill-hole or other, to keep my mouth from speaking. (p. 63)

This quote illustrates how compulsive scruples may be both *acts* (clapping his hand over his mouth) and *thoughts* (the idea of jumping into a hole). When he had the obsession to give in to the temptation to "sell Christ," he notes his resistance in physical acts (compulsions):

> ...I have been forced to stand as continually leaning and forcing my spirit against it, lest haply, before I were aware, some wicked thought might arise in my heart, that might consent thereto.... (p.79)

On another occasion—

> ...in labouring to gainsay and resist this wickedness, my very body would be put into action or motion, by way of pushing or thrusting with my hands or elbows. (p.79)[7]

But his resistance is to no avail. Indeed, the obsession *becomes all-pervasive.*

> But it was neither my dislike of the thought, nor yet any desire and endeavor to resist, that in the least did shake or abate the continuation or force and strength thereof; ...I

could neither eat my food, stoop for a pin, chop a stick, or cast mine eye to look on this or that, but still the temptation would come, *Sell Christ for this, or sell Christ for that; sell Him, sell Him.* (pp.78-79, italics in original)

He deftly describes two clinical features seen in the condition: *anxiety and depression.* Anxiety interferes with his concentration:

If I have been reading, then sometimes I had sudden thoughts to question all I read; sometimes again, my mind would be so strangely snatched away, and possessed with other things, that I have neither known, nor regarded, nor remembered so much as the sentence that but now I have read. (pp.64-65)

The deepest state of clinical depression is characterized by *no longer having a capacity to cry.*[8]

And now my heart was, at times, exceeding hard; if I would have given a thousand pounds for a tear, I could not shed one: no nor sometimes scarce desire to shed one. (p.64)

Bunyan also experiences the healing effect of *sharing his problem* with someone who suffered in the same way.

About this time I took an opportunity to break my mind to an ancient Christian, and told him all my case: I told him also, that I was afraid that I had sinned the sin against the Holy Ghost; and he told me, *He thought so too....* (p.101, italics in original)

He notes, ironically, that he took "cold comfort" from this person's self-disclosure, yet it was insufficient, and he turned back to seeking assurance from prayer. Later, after he overcomes his scruples, Bunyan observes that no one can truly understand the torment of scruples nor the peace of their absence unless experienced personally.

None but those that know what my trouble (by their own experience) was, can tell what relief came to my soul by this consideration. (p.108)

This highlights the usefulness of sharing the condition with fellow sufferers. Unfortunately, the unusual nature of the obsessions and compulsions prevent people with scruples or OCD from actively seeking out others.[9]

Another feature Bunyan portrays fits in well with modern clinical observations. The idea that certain types of thoughts are dangerous characterizes scruples and OCD.[10] People come to this notion in different ways—perhaps by instruction (modeling), perhaps by experience. Bunyan describes an intriguing event which may provide a clue as to how he became especially sensitized to the power of his thoughts. Once, when his wife was advanced in pregnancy, she started to have severe labor pains, but apparently prematurely. As she lay in pain crying beside him, Bunyan narrates his touching prayer to God for her.

> *Lord, if Thou wilt now remove this sad affliction from my wife, and cause that she be troubled no more therewith this night* (and now were her pangs just upon her), *then I shall know that Thou canst discern the most secret thoughts of the heart.* (p.134, italics in original)

Bunyan reports that no sooner had he prayed than her pains were removed from her and she fell into a peaceful sleep until morning. This made a powerful impression:

> ...how the Lord had showed me, that He knew my secret thoughts, which was a great astonishment to me.... (p.135)

Although many religions teach that God knows our innermost thoughts, this experience may have helped sensitize Bunyan to its truth for him, so that God would know even a fleeting idea or image, and unacceptable ones could be cause for judgment.

*Conclusion.* I have explored Bunyan's process, not only because of his articulate and ancient description of a modern problem, but because it touches on nearly every aspect of scruples. We see all the major issues displayed: scrupulous obsessions with undoing compulsions (thoughts, acts), the need to resist, the pervasive nature of the obsessions, the resultant anxiety and depression, the notion that some thoughts are dangerous, the limited relief from sharing with fellow-sufferers, and the insidious nature of the obsessions which defy logic or the person's own value system.

Bunyan does not help us much, however, with a solution, or at least with a solution that will have universal appeal or efficacy. Eventually, through prayer and scripture reading, he obtained reassurance from his doubts and obsessions. Certainly Bunyan views this reassurance as the gift of grace, and aptly names his book *Grace Abounding*.

From the outside we certainly see little logic to what finally brings relief. His whole life was consumed with searching the Bible and praying for the right answer. I found it curious that some texts, which appeared quite relevant to his doubts, provided only temporary relief; but other texts, which appear tangential at best, provided permanent relief. The theologian might say here that Bunyan was being "prepared" through these endeavors to accept grace, and indeed the actual text or moment would seem minor.

Another well-known religious figure with scruples is St. Ignatius Loyola, founder of the Jesuits. Shortly after his conversion to the spiritual life from the life of a soldier, he experienced severe scruples. He doubted that his past sins were truly forgiven, and compulsively examined his conscience for hours at a time. He had the urge to repeat past sins in confession, and would doubt the adequacy of his confessions. Like Bunyan, his torment was so great that he was driven to the brink of suicide.[11]

As we will note in the next chapter, he was relieved from the scruples through the standard pastoral care strategy passed down through the centuries, i.e. reliance on a firm spiritual guide. His confessor told him not to confess his past sins anymore.

> He therefore made up his mind, which had become very clear on the matter, never to confess his past sins again, and from that day on he remained free of those scruples, holding it a certainty that our Lord in his mercy had liberated him.[12]

This reliance on a spiritual guide arises out of the desperation the person with scruples feels. To escape the religious torment drives some to extreme measures. Both Bunyan and Ignatius considered suicide. The prayer of Ignatius could echo the despair of those with scruples.

> Show me, Lord, where I can obtain help: and if I have to follow a little dog to obtain the cure I need, I am ready to do just that.[13]

One religious commentator holds that spiritual solutions to scrupulosity are possible when they have powerful emotional aspects and are not limited to absorption of factual information.[14] This may explain how Bunyan found some scripture passages reassuring but others irrelevant. Although Bunyan was a great admirer of Martin Luther, the famous passage from Romans that resolved Luther's concern about salvation was insufficient for Bunyan.

But most people troubled by scruples are like those of us who try to help them—ordinary people, not spiritual giants. As a clinician, I feel obligated to push beyond Bunyan, Ignatius, and Luther's solution, the way a surgeon who believes in miracles might try to heal a deformed leg. We have no data on how often prayer alone relieves scruples, and so it seems useful to explore other avenues, especially since we see the failure of prayer alone in most cases of scruples in OCD. We are reminded of the adage, "Pray as if everything depends on God; act as if everything depends on you."

The number and variety of religious scruples defy imagination. I have prepared a list of a sampling of the content of moral or religious scruples which I have encountered in clinical practice or supervision (Figure 3-1). Although one can spot common themes, e.g. honesty, aggression, etc., the *specific* content may be highly unusual and unpredictable. I am constantly hearing about new twists in the content of scruples. The list may also suggest why sufferers are reluctant to share their feelings and impulses.

Before we move on to discussing psychological and pastoral strategies for relieving scruples, we will look briefly at how religious tradition has approached the problem of scruples over the centuries.

**Figure 3-1 List of Scruples**

The following are examples of obsessions and compulsions in religiously committed persons with OCD who were in outpatient treatment.

| THEME | OBSESSION | COMPULSION |
|---|---|---|
| Honesty | 1) Grocery store cashier may have made an error *in favor* of the patient. | 1) Receipts are taken home and laboriously checked item by item, even if totals involve hundreds of dollars. Some receipts are kept for months, with the patient hoping that the urge to check will eventually decline and he can throw them away. |
| | 2) Urge to touch produce in grocery store triggers obsessions that this would "damage" the food, making it unsuitable for other shoppers to buy. This would be the equivalent of stealing, since it defrauds the store. | 2) Will examine produce only visually, and feels compelled to purchase any item touched. |
| Blasphemy | 1) Impulse to make obscene gesture at God. | 1) Touch face seven times with middle finger of each hand each time impulse occurs. |

| THEME | OBSESSION | COMPULSION |
|---|---|---|
| Blasphemy (continued) | | 2) Repeat prayers for 30-60 minutes to "atone" for the impulse. |
| | 2) Impulse to curse God. | |
| | 3) Impulse to take off clothes in church. | 3) Only goes to church with friends or family members. |
| Cooperation in Sin | 1) Unmarried couple discusses taking cruise together. Person hears this and concludes she has sinned by not confronting the couple about their presumed immorality. | 1) Seeks reassurance that she has not sinned from clergyperson. |
| | 2) Man participates in discussion about a historical figure dead for over 1000 years, who is alleged to have been homosexual. He worries that he has committed the sin of "detraction." | 2) Seeks reassurance that he has not sinned from clergyperson. |
| | 3) Woman sees golf foursome several hundred yards behind. She does not "warn" her partner about the foursome, | 3) Seeks reassurance from clergyperson. |

| THEME | OBSESSION | COMPULSION |
|---|---|---|
| Cooperation in Sin (continued) | and concludes she has sinned by failing to alert her partner to get out of harm's way. | |
| Sexual Ideas | 1) Woman worries about being homosexual. | 1) Seeks reassurance from numerous clergy and mental health professionals. |
| | 2) Man has image of touching his child's genitals when diapering or bathing the baby. | 2) Long series of prayers to "become right" with God for "forbidden" impulses. |
| | 3) Man experiences sexual arousal in middle of night upon awakening briefly. Worries that he is "consenting" to sexual impurity. | 3) Remains motionless for as long as an hour to prevent any movement that might be viewed as enhancing the arousal. |
| Aggression | 1) Idea that woman may have murdered strange children in her sleep. | 1) Seeks reassurance from her spouse that she remained in bed all night. |
| | 2) Belief that driving the car will cause injury to pedestrians. | 2) Drive no faster than 25 mph on all streets and highways. |

| THEME | OBSESSION | COMPULSION |
|---|---|---|
| Aggression (continued) | 3) Pass teenage boy on crowded city street. Belief that he may have mortally wounded the boy by brushing against him. | 3) Walks around the area of encounter for 20 minutes attempting to locate youngster. |
| | 4) Driver goes over a bump on interstate highway at night. Believes that the bump could have been a person. | 4) Drives seven miles to the next exit, circles back, pulls the car off the highway, and searches for the body for 30 minutes. |
| | 5) Mother worries that blankets, electrical extension cords, belts, neckwear, knives, and hot water are potential objects for her to asault her infant. | 5) She hides the objects or stays out of any room that has them. |
| | 6) Father worries that ordinary rough-housing with his two year old will physically injure the child. | 6) Repeatedly examines child for evidence of physical injury. |
| Charity | 1) Parent worries that child does not know parent truly loves her. | 1) Repeats "I love you" dozens of times when putting child to sleep. |
| | 2) Worker worries that he must show | 2) Greets every person he passes in the |

| THEME | OBSESSION | COMPULSION |
|---|---|---|
| Charity (continued) | "love of neighbor" to all employees in his twelve-story government building. | corridor. |
| | 3) Woman attends wake of friend's spouse. Worries that she will inadvertently smile during the services, thereby showing disrespect. | 3) Keeps hand over mouth during entire service. |
| Death | 1) Concern that God will cause the person's death at an early age in retaliation for past sins. | 1) Frequent prayers to avoid God's wrath. |
| Harm/Injury | 1) Image of spouse dying in fatal crash. | 1) Prays two to three hours nightly to prevent the tragedy. |
| | 2) Chemistry teacher sees spots on dress pants. Worries that they could be poisonous chemicals. | 2) Refuses to have pants dry cleaned for fear of harming garment workers. |
| | 3) Nurse worries he will miscalculate medications and injure patient. | 3) Checks dosage frequently. Eventually gives up nursing. |

| THEME | OBSESSION | COMPULSION |
|---|---|---|
| Miscellaneous Doubts | 1) Idea intrudes on man that he may not truly have human freedom, but all his actions are determined. | 1) Regularly blurts out unusual, negative statements unexpectedly, just to "prove that he can exercise free will." |

*Chapter 4*

---

# Scruples in the History of Pastoral Care

## Introduction

Our discussion to this point indicates the long literary history and clinical experience with OCD symptoms we know as scruples. Scruples have a long pastoral and theological tradition as well. The methods which evolved to provide spiritual, humane care to people with scruples in their journey toward salvation allow us to dissect the underlying psychological principles in light of modern knowledge. We will see how some of these pastoral care strategies anticipated, by centuries, the principles of behavior therapy developed to treat OCD.

Scrupulosity presented a challenge to the church's thinkers at two different but related levels. On the theoretical level scrupulosity was interesting in itself as an issue in moral reasoning. Moral theology in the Catholic Church developed in the early Middle Ages in the universities in a highly refined, systematic manner. Moral theology treatises discussed scrupulosity under the section on "conscience." The dilemma for moral theology in this framework was, "To what degree is a scrupulous conscience a correct one?" Moral theology held that people are obligated to follow their conscience, but that a person has an obligation to *inform* his or her conscience (i.e. bring it into conformity with objectively correct behavior).

What were scrupulous persons to do? On the one hand, they must follow their conscience. On the other hand, doubt is the essence of scrupulosity. The general rule for moral action was, "No one can act with a doubtful conscience." First, resolve the doubt in some way.[1] How is it possible to resolve a doubt logically when a person constantly *feels* doubtful?

To solve the quandary theologians applied the principle of an *erro-*

*neous conscience.* By definition, an erroneous conscience was one that was not in conformity with the objective reality of a moral act. It either viewed moral acts as wrong or immoral acts as right. In the case of scrupulosity the person sees sin where there is none. Labeling a scrupulous conscience as erroneous was liberating for the person. Since an erroneous conscience could not "bind" a person to follow its direction, *a scrupulous person is free to act without resolving the doubt.*

The theologian says in essence that a person with a scrupulous conscience judges a particular moral act incorrectly, and, therefore, the act does not have the moral meaning the person *feels* he or she may have intended. This resolution provided a practical solution for the scrupulous person and the church used this idea to develop pastoral strategies for support. The strategies, in effect, were exemptions to laws and practices required of the non-scrupulous. What is particularly intriguing from the modern perspective is that these principles were well formulated as early as the fifteenth and sixteenth centuries. In attempting to solve a spiritual problem for its members, these writings document the ancient existence of a troubling emotional condition.

When it came to pastoral care of the scrupulous, the church applied these moral theology principles in a number of practical ways. We can get a sense of the culmination of this tradition in a clerical best-seller on moral theology used for training priests.[2] This manual reflects moral theology in seminary training up to the eve of the Second Vatican Council (1962-65), which altered many aspects of Catholic practice and education.[3]

Writing in the middle of this century, the authors incorporate both the ancient theology tradition and the insights of current psychology. "The basic factor in a scrupulous conscience is not so much error as fear." (p.38) They describe the anxieties as not rational in character. They also observe, as have clinicians, that a person might be scrupulous in one area but lax in others. (Recall the example earlier of the person with a cleaning and praying ritual after masturbation, yet who regularly visited prostitutes.)

They list as the causes what today we would call biological, personality and character influences. "Organic" causes include manic-depressive impulses, pressure on the brain, anemia, and abnormal irritability. This predates current brain explanations described in Chapter 2 (e.g. the serotonin hypothesis). Personality factors include vivid fantasies, excessive feeling in proportion to thinking, and excessive introspection. Character defects include secret pride or a lack of confidence in divine mercy.

The authors' guidelines for personal behavior anticipate many of the components of behavior therapy treatment for OCD. If the scrupulous desire to act morally, they need to disregard the scruples. "There is even a *duty* to act contrary to scruples, for one might otherwise sin by pride, self-will and disobedience." (p.42, italics in original)

They make several practical suggestions. 1) Copy the behavior of conscientious people even if doing so makes the person feel uncomfortable (modeling).[4] 2) If the person has "impure" thoughts when looking at innocent persons or objects, he or she is allowed to "look attentively at such things and becomingly at such persons and pay no attention to the resultant emotions." (p.42) We described this behavioral strategy as exposure. 3) In the arena of the sacrament of confession, confessors are to forbid the scrupulous from repeating confessions, no matter how doubtful the penitent is that he or she has made a "good" confession: i.e. has enumerated each and every serious sin (blocking). 4) The behavioral method of exposure is further mirrored in recommending that the scrupulous follow their spiritual director's advice faithfully, "even at the risk of making an occasional mistake."

These guidelines adjust pastoral practice in a way that respects tradition, yet reduces the burden. This flexibility even extends to relieving the scrupulous from duties incumbent on others. They need not "fraternally correct." That is, their oversensitivity to sin would result in their misjudging others' behavior, yet the scrupulous might feel obligated to confront people constantly. Naturally, such actions would destroy relationships and ultimately be an offense against charity. So, rather than obsessing constantly about whether, when and whom to correct, they are simply dispensed from this obligation. As noted above, they are also dispensed from confessional "integrity," i.e. the obligation to enumerate each and every type of serious sin. They alone are permitted to describe their serious sins in a general way without a number count. Finally, they should not repeat prayers or obligatory worship (e.g. on Sunday) even if they believe they were "distracted" at the time.

## Scruples versus Religious Practice

Freud, and others, have noted the similarity between religious rituals and defense mechanisms.[5] The mental health field today, however, requires integration or, at a minimum, respect for personal faith. At the same time, faith communities are now more discriminating about the potential dangers of some forms of belief. They are aware that some religious systems harm the individual or the community. Some authors provide guidelines to distinguish "true" from "false" religion. Others highlight the dangers with titles such as *Toxic Faith*, or *When God Becomes a Drug.*[6]

The mental health professional, as well as the person with scruples, does not always have a theological background to distinguish valid religious practices from scruples. The person with scruples, due to the nature of the problem, is often not in a position to make the judgment. Seldom will the treatment professional share the exact religious background of the person seeking help. I have also found that even when the religious background is shared, the person with scruples is not necessarily reassured. Endless debates may result, if the professional allows, about what is a "liberal" or "conservative" position, and whether you will lead them down the garden path of destruction.

Psychiatrist David Greenberg enumerates five principles for distinguishing normal from pathological religious principles.[7]

1) Compulsive behavior goes beyond the requirements of religious law. These are practices that are "more Catholic than the pope." If rules of fasting call for no food or drink, scruples become obsessions about not swallowing saliva (as if this were physically possible).

2) Compulsive behavior has a narrow focus. Persons may direct their attention to one aspect of religious experience, but exclude others—for example, spending all their energy avoiding sexual misconduct.

3) In a similar vein, compulsive behavior often focuses on what is trivial to religious practice. A person may worry about allowing holy water to fall on the floor when making the sign of the cross upon entering the church.

4) As a result of scruples' narrow focus, important areas of religious life are ignored. The person may be rigid about external rituals, but pays little attention to commandments relating to love of neighbor.

5) Scruples resemble the compulsions of OCD, in that repeating and checking play a prominent role. Major religions prohibit, either by law or custom, repeating prayers or rituals.

## Conclusions

We can draw several principles for the care of scruples from the pastoral tradition reviewed in this chapter.

1) To avoid psychological and moral paralysis, the person has a duty to act contrary to the scruples. This notion of *doing the opposite* of scrupulous urges forms the foundation of exposure treatment for OCD developed by behavior therapists. In the sixteenth century, St. Ignatius Loyola, founder of the Jesuits, wrote this same principle as a guide for overcoming scruples in his famous manual on spiritual development, *The Spiritual Exercises.*[8] The principle became a proverb for spiritual direction, and was stated in Latin as *agere contra*, do the opposite.

2) The scrupulous person is permitted to use the behavior of conscientious persons as models for moral behavior, and follow their example without tedious moral reasoning.

3) The person with scruples should follow the guidance of a single spiritual director blindly. Jumping from one religious guide to another is forbidden.

4) One may and should place oneself directly in situations or circumstances which trigger the scruples.

5) One may not repeat religious rituals or prayers, nor let them function in any way as compulsions.

These principles, over four hundred years old, contain the seeds of modern behavioral treatments. Naturally, they are not systematically elaborated, nor did the authors have a premonition of classical conditioning. Nevertheless, we see the heart of learning theory strategies used to treat OCD: modeling, exposure to the upsetting situation, and blocking the compulsive response.[9]

In the next section we attempt to combine insights from this pastoral tradition with those of behavioral strategies for fear reduction.[10]

# Part Two

# CHANGING SCRUPLES

*Chapter 5*

# Targeting Scruples and Developing Motivation

The three chapters in Part Two form the heart of change strategies for scruples. We will draw on both modern psychological principles as well as the tradition of pastoral care for this endeavor. In this chapter we will focus first on identifying the person's relevant scruples which require change.

Mere intellectual insight, however, is not enough to generate change. Most people with scruples have a sense of what is wrong, and can even identify their own distortions. When a treatment plan is outlined, however, fear, anxiety and confusion may take over. The plan is either never attempted or abandoned early. We shall spend considerable time on practical suggestions for generating motivation to change, rather than leaving this important psychological dimension to chance (or the sin of presumption!).

## Targeting Scruples for Change

The first struggle, then, is identifying what needs to change. To complete this task we need to review briefly the two main components of the condition. Each component requires identification because the strategy differs for each. What we call targeting scruples is a task known to the clinician as *assessment*. This process is essential, as my old speech teacher liked to say about the necessity of preparation: "If you aim at nothing, you're bound to hit it."

Scruples involve both obsessions and compulsions. We will modify the traditional psychiatric formulation slightly which defined obsessions as recurrent, unwanted ideas, and compulsions as recurrent unwanted acts. Instead we will rely on the behaviorists' functional definitions, since they are clearer and easier to work with. In the revised functional definition obsessions are repeated thoughts, images, urges or acts which *trigger* anxiety. Compulsions are repeated acts, thoughts, or images which *reduce* anxiety.[1] This formulation recognizes that mental activity (e.g. thoughts or images) can operate as compulsions just as behavior can. This definition fits scruples better because many scruples are *mental* compulsions, e.g. repeating prayers in one's mind to undo a non-existent "sin."

*Distinguishing Scruples from Worries.* How do scruples differ from normal worries? Worry in the general population usually includes themes related to family, finances, occupation or health. Scruples may include these themes, but they differ in several ways. They are *frequent.* They have high *intensity.* They *last much longer.* The *quality* of the scruple is usually more horrible in its imagery or imagined outcome. Finally, people usually want to *undo* or *resist* obsessional scruples. They feel an urge to neutralize it.

*Identifying Obsessional Scruples.* The skill required to identify scruples is *self-monitoring.* The person must pay attention to the obsessions and compulsions with a degree of detachment, as if he were an outside observer keeping a record. No hard and fast rule exists on how to do this. Keeping a written record probably is most helpful, but need not be the only one. My own clients who make the effort to keep records usually make the most rapid progress. I provide examples of record-keeping in this chapter and the next two. The reader should feel free to use and copy them, or create forms.

What, then, should the person self-observe? As the forms suggest, self-observation involves several parts: the obsessions themselves, the compulsions themselves, the intensity of the anxiety, and the circumstances in which the obsessions and compulsions occur.

Most people with scruples, but not all, will have both obsessions and compulsions. Reading through this material should clarify the picture, or the person should seek guidance if still unsure. Since obsessions trigger the anxiety, we begin by identifying them.

First, pay attention to the worries themselves. What exactly are they? Recall from Chapter 3 the typical content of obsessions. Are the themes sexual, blasphemous, aggressive (I might cause harm to someone), embarrassing (smiling at a sad story), honesty (took something of value, cheated on income tax), illness/death (loved ones or self), or doubts about committing a sin (listened to gossip)? A list of common obsessions called the Yale-Brown Obsessive Compulsive Symptom

Checklist is provided in Appendix B. This list can help identify prob-lem areas, or the reader may refer back to the examples in Chapter 4.

The obsession (if it truly is one) also triggers a particular worry. The person does not want the idea because the idea will result in one of the following: 1) unwanted acts, 2) unwanted speech, or 3) unwanted feel-ings.[2] Some people worry that the obsession will trigger misconduct (e.g. sexual misbehavior). Others worry about an urge to say something reprehensible (e.g. make an obscene phone call). Other obsessions are troublesome because they generate doubt and guilt (e.g. did I injure or steal from someone?).

Obsessions, then, give rise to worries about these unwanted reac-tions. Notice that the emphasis is on the idea of *unwanted* not necessar-ily *painful* or *unpleasant* ideas or urges. Some of the unwanted acts or feelings might be pleasurable but the person opposes experiencing them (e.g. sexual or aggressive feelings).

The person begins by identifying four or five of the most noticeable obsessions. Identify those which take up the most time either through time spent worrying or in attempts to neutralize them. Identify, also, those which interfere with other requirements of daily life: occupation, family, recreation, and household responsibilities.

Specify as clearly as possible *what the unwanted act, speech or feel-ing is* (e.g. hurting my baby, consenting to blasphemy). Some clients tell me that they are not always sure what the fear is. They report a sud-den fear that some act will trigger a vague sense of guilt. For example, turning on a light switch at home may have some unpermitted sexual meaning. Figure 5-1 is one example of a self-monitoring record for obsessional scruples. Figure 5-2 is an example of monitoring scruples with themes such as anger, honesty and blasphemy.

Some self-observers can distinguish obsessions from compulsions almost immediately. They will prefer to record both as they begin self-monitoring. Others will experience the scruples in a confusing jumble. Just begin recording in either the obsession or compulsion column at first if confused. The differences usually clear up later. The change strategies still work if total clarity is impossible.

A warning for all self-monitors! *Do not turn the self-recording itself into another compulsion.* Sometimes when I have asked clients to keep records between sessions, they return with thirty to forty written pages. The emphasis here is on quality not quantity. Limit recording to one or two pages daily. This provides more than enough useful information.

**Figure 5-1**
**Daily Record of Obsessions and Compulsions**

| Date | Situation | OBSESSION:<br><br>Thought, image, impulse or behavior that *triggers* anxiety | Tension Level 1 - 10 | COMPULSION:<br><br>Thought, image, impulse or behavior that *reduces* anxiety | Time spent dealing with obsession and/or compulsion |
|------|-----------|-----------|-----------|-----------|-----------|
|      | *Describe* | *Describe* |  | *Describe* |  |

**Figure 5-2**

**Daily Record of Obsessions and Compulsions**

| Date | Situation | OBSESSION: Thought, image, impulse or behavior that *triggers* anxiety | Tension Level 1 - 10 | COMPULSION: Thought, image, impulse or behavior that *reduces* anxiety | Time spent dealing with obsession and/or compulsion |
|---|---|---|---|---|---|
| Mon. | *Describe* Angry with spouse; did not help with dishes | *Describe* God will punish me by taking my spouse | 9 | *Describe* Prayed two hours to God not to take spouse | 120 minutes |
| Tues. | Saw attractive person | Worried I had impure thought | 8 | Asked reassurance from minister | Spoke to minister three times about this |
| | Gave plumber cash for fixing leak | I am accessory to tax fraud, if plumber does not declare it on annual taxes | 7 | Called my accountant for reassurance | Ten minute conversation |

**Figure 5-2 (continued)**
**Daily Record of Obsessions and Compulsions**

| Date | Situation | OBSESSION: | Tension Level 1 - 10 | COMPULSION: | Time spent dealing with obsession |
|---|---|---|---|---|---|
| Wed. | While saying night prayer | Idea comes that God is really the Evil One | 10 | Tried to "think it through" as a theological idea. Looked up Bible quotes and religious writings | Four hours |

From:  Joseph W. Ciarrocchi, Ph.D.
*The Doubting Disease*
Paulist Press

Copy worksheet for personal or therapeutic use.

*Identifying Compulsive Scruples.* Compulsions are the acts, thoughts, or images which reduce the anxiety triggered by the obsession. Compulsions are sometimes tricky to name since they may take two forms which are functionally different. First, some compulsions are *elaborate acts* or rituals which are meant to neutralize the obsession. Saying prayers, cleaning house, going to confession, and seeking reassurance that no injury was done are all examples of this type. Other compulsions are *avoidance acts* which are meant to prevent some unwanted outcome. Keeping eyes downcast in public so as not to view anything that triggers an impure thought, and carrying bags in both hands when crossing a street to prevent acting on the impulse to strike other pedestrians are examples of avoidance compulsions. Understanding how each compulsion functions is important when using the strategy of doing the opposite.

Chapter 3 provides extensive examples of compulsive scruples, if the reader needs to identify common patterns. Briefly, they may include checking to see if something was done correctly, seeking reassurance from others, repeating behavior to clarify doubts, and making complicated attempts to arrange one's environment to resist unpleasant or embarrassing urges. I cannot emphasize enough that the content of obsessional and compulsive scruples is potentially infinite. I hear unique ones nearly each time I work with a new client. The task is to identify the scruple's function.

*Record Circumstances Surrounding the Scruples.* To understand scruples more fully, the person needs to know what situations, events, or circumstances trigger the scruples. Careful monitoring of the situations makes it easier to predict when the scruples will occur. This permits establishing precise strategies to eliminate the scruples.

The situation or circumstances may be either *internal* or *external* events. External events include people, places or things surrounding you when scruples occur. Or the triggering events may be an idea that "comes out of the blue," that does not seem influenced by the environment. For example, when brushing his teeth John worries about his children's safety on the school bus. Brushing teeth is not central to triggering the obsession. But even when internal events seem to trigger scruples, knowledge of the environment often provides useful information.

What circumstances, then, should one describe? I suggest the phrases from journalism class that ensure the reporter covers the essential details of a story. Who, what, when, where, why, how often, how many, and how much? Answering one or more of these questions when filling out the situation column should provide the necessary information. Note the examples on the sample record (Figure 5-2).

Recording the *intensity* of the anxiety helps assessment. A short-hand method to describe the degree of anxiety is a simple scale from one to ten. One represents total lack of anxiety and ten equals total fear. An example of ten is the amount of fear generated if your foot is stuck in a railroad track and a train whistle sounds around the bend.

The *amount of time* spent worrying about or coping with obsessions and compulsions also provides valuable information. In the beginning this helps distinguish major from minor scruples. Scruples often come in large bundles, so that tracking intensity of the anxiety and amount of time spent dealing with them can help sort out which to tackle first. We will suggest tackling minor scruples first to develop self-confidence. But only accurate self-observation can separate minor from major ones. Again, the sample record (Figure 5-2) provides examples of scruples that vary by intensity and time consumed.

*Putting It All Together.* If the person stays committed to self-monitoring, consistent themes will emerge. Similar obsessional and compulsive scruples recur. The final step, then, is to summarize the most frequent scruples (both obsessional and compulsive) into four or five types. This includes recording scruples that are high and low in intensity and the amount of time spent coping.

I have provided a summary record to tally the target obsessions and compulsions (Figures 5-3, 5-4). Leave space on the summary record to list new scruples as they are attended to. Although two to three weeks of self-observation usually suffices to pick out main themes, some become apparent only after the change strategies commence. This is normal, and the later discoveries are added to the list for future consideration.

Before applying the change strategies, reflecting on the necessity of change may be required to develop the motivation to carry out the next difficult phase.

## Motivation to Change: Or, Have You Had Enough Yet?

Too often when people begin a self-change project they move immediately from assessment to change tactics. This is particularly true for

**Figure 5-3**
**Target Obsessions List**

**OBSESSION:** Thought, image, impulse or behavior that *triggers* anxiety.

Average Tension
Level

1. _____
2. _____
3. _____
4. _____
5. _____
6. _____
7. _____
8. _____
9. _____
10. _____

**Tension Level**
1      = No anxiety
2-3    = Mild anxiety
4-5    = Moderate anxiety
6-7    = Severe anxiety
8-10  = Intense anxiety

**Guidelines:**
Work first on obsession that generates *least* amount of tension, on average. (Do not obsess if some are very close. Pick any one, flip a coin, etc.)

From: Joseph W. Ciarrocchi, Ph.D.
        *The Doubting Disease*
        Paulist Press

Copy worksheet for personal or therapeutic use.

**Figure 5-4**
**Target Compulsions List**

**COMPULSIONS:** Thought, image, impulse or behavior that
*reduces* anxiety.

Average Tension
Level

1. _____
2. _____
3. _____
4. _____
5. _____
6. _____
7. _____
8. _____
9. _____
10. _____

**Tension Level**
1     = No anxiety
2-3   = Mild anxiety
4-5   = Moderate anxiety
6-7   = Severe anxiety
8-10 = Intense anxiety

**Guidelines:**
Work first on compulsion
that generates *least* amount
of tension, on average. (Do
not obsess if some are very
close.)

From: Joseph W. Ciarrocchi, Ph.D.
       *The Doubting Disease*
       Paulist Press

Copy worksheet for
personal or therapeutic use.

behaviors which we popularly label compulsive: dieting, alcohol use, drugs, a sedentary life-style, etc. This method is ineffective. A study of persons making New Year's resolutions, for example, found that 60 percent abandoned them within six months.[3] Psychologists now recognize from research data what the average person long understood. That is, people generally know *what to do* if they want to change a habit or behavior pattern. Sometimes they are unclear on how to change. But most often failure to change is based on weak motivation.

The problem is even greater when the target of change involves some form of mental control, as in the case of scruples. A large body of evidence demonstrates that the more we try to *not* think about something, the greater the attraction it has. Ask any recovering alcoholic how successful he or she was in the early days of sobriety in forcing out images of wanting to take a drink. Clearly, motivation is not the same thing as will power, since will power only involves intending to change.

A new theory of change has been proposed to assess the person's current motivation to change, and to provide means for increasing motivation. The model grew out of trying to understand how we go about changing compulsive behaviors such as overeating, excessive alcohol use, drug use, procrastination and other types of "bad habits."[4] This model proposes five stages in the change process.

*Precontemplation.* In this stage the person may have fleeting thoughts such as, "It would be nice if I did something about this problem," or, "I think I'll look into what I need to do about this sometime." No serious consideration of change exists during this stage of the problem. People with scruples at this stage would view scruples as something they "have" to do, and they would not even remotely consider the possibility of investigating change. That is probably not true for persons who have approached an advisor to discuss their problem.

*Contemplation.* In this stage *ambivalence* is the core feature. The person has powerful reasons and feelings for both change *and* no change. A boyhood friend from the rural southern United States called ambivalent people "mugwumps." In colloquial Americanese a mugwump is a person who sits on a fence with his mug on one side and his wump on the other. Psychologist William Miller, in only a slightly more sophisticated analogy, uses the image of a playground seesaw to describe this stage. In the contemplation stage the person resembles a see-saw perfectly balanced in mid-air. For every reason to change, the person has an equally strong reason not to change. This balance is experienced as ambivalence and results in paralysis.

This stage characterizes many with scruples. They are clearly aware that a serious problem exists. Yet the negatives of change predominate; e.g. fear, the uncertainty of living in doubt, the lack of a support system, lack of trust in advisors, etc. The person continues to investigate remedies, talk to authorities, or read about the problem, but no decision to change is actually made.

*Determination.* In this stage the person makes a clear *decision.* The decision takes different forms: "I've had enough of this; I am going to do whatever it takes to change." In this stage the person *makes an act of the will* to change the behavior. In other words, the person describes a direct *intention* to change. At this point a clear resolution is framed: "I am going to stop drinking"; "I am going on a diet tomorrow"; "I will begin an exercise program." In the case of scruples the person comes to believe the scruples are senseless, or at least need to be eliminated. The person may say, "I am going to stop giving in to them," or, "I am going to get help for this."

*Action.* In western society and in many religious cultures will power is oversold. Many believe that most, if not all, habits can change through an act of the will, i.e. through a *decision* to change. Research and life experience tell us otherwise. Over fifty years ago, Alcoholics Anonymous (AA) developed a successful self-help fellowship for severe alcoholics with a strategy directly opposite to the use of will power. AA realized that just because a person wants to change, even if the desire is enormous, he or she will not have the necessary personal skills to bring about change.[5]

Almost all behavior change, particularly compulsions, require several different skills to accomplish. The following represent the core ingredients:

1) Information about the compulsion.
2) Analysis of the situations triggering the person's compulsion.
3) Cognitive and behavioral skills available to establish alternative, competing behaviors to the compulsion.
4) Social supports which will enhance changes rather than maintain the prior undesired behavior.

In this stage the person undertakes an action plan. An ineffective plan results in immediate relapse and discouragement. With repeated relapse and no technical adjustment to the plan, hopelessness is inevitable and the plan is abandoned. This reinforces for the person that "nothing works," and "motivation" dies.

The message for coping with scruples, then, is that past failure to remedy them does not mean the person is weak-willed or hopeless. Rather, the person simply has lacked some essential ingredients for effective change. Further, the person *can learn* these skills with patience and proper direction.

*Maintenance.* Because relapse is universal when changing long-standing habits, any effective change plan requires a maintenance strategy. No habit changes immediately. Only repeated success guarantees elimination. Research suggests that early discouragement reduces the probability of renewed attempts. Yet, ironically, those who successfully overcome addictions, for example, are those *who had repeated failures attempting to stop.* The trick, then, is to view each lapse as one step along the road to permanent success. Unfortunately, many will view any setback with discouragement, hopelessness and helplessness.

A maintenance strategy *anticipates* lapses, plans for them, and suggests methods for handling them. Imagine that I have decided to begin an exercise program and set aside thirty minutes each morning after I wake up. Further, I have now succeeded in my program for three weeks. On Tuesday morning I feel that I may be coming down with a cold, so I reset my alarm back to 7:00 A.M. On Wednesday I realize that I am not sick, after all, but probably was just a little tired. However, I failed to reset my alarm and missed a second day also. Now I am at a crossroads. I have lost my momentum and could easily go back permanently to my old rising time.

A maintenance strategy plans for such events, and has back-up plans available as needed. In this case I may ask my eleven year old child who gets up with the chickens to wake me up. The same concept holds for changing scruples, and we discuss this more fully in Chapter 6.

## A Personal Motivation Plan

Each person with scruples needs to develop his or her personal motivation for change. The focus of this section is to help overcome ambivalence about the necessity to change.

Let's return to the image of the playground seesaw. Prior to taking effective action, the person views reasons for change about the same as reasons for not changing. Most of the reasons for change relate more to fear than to actual conviction. Nevertheless, fear is a powerful motivator to maintain the present situation. As a result, the person is balanced in mid-air on the seesaw, ill-at-ease with both positions.

"Motivation" means placing weights on the side of the balance to provide incentives for change. The person needs to focus on *the negative effects and drawbacks* of scruples. Since doubt and fear drive the scruples, the person already is keenly aware of the pain involved in eliminating them. To increase motivation the person needs also to focus on *the positive aspects of change.*

The Personal Motivation List in Figure 5-5 can assist this process. Once when I introduced this grid to a nun client, her eyes brightened. She informed me that she used this regularly in her retreat work and spiritual renewal workshops. She had learned it from spiritual guides in the tradition of St. Ignatius Loyola. I thought my "discovery" came from motivational psychology.[6]

The grid consists of two parts. First, the "pros," i.e. positive reasons to change scruples. Second, the "cons," i.e. the negatives if the person does *not* change. Naturally, if persons are interested in change, they should emphasize the first category, since they are already well acquainted with the drive not to change.

Under reasons for change chart two categories. First, list the *benefits* of change (see Figure 5-6). In the case of scruples, the benefits include more free time, a greater sense of freedom, more quality time with family members, etc. Next, list the *costs* of not changing. These may include loss of freedom, my children looking at me strangely, personal embarrassment, interference with my occupation or job, an inability to enjoy certain leisure activities, reduced participation in religious activities, etc.

Take considerable time to make the list complete. If you keep self-monitoring records, they can provide many examples of the costs of not changing and the benefits of change. In listing reasons for change be sure to enumerate examples that have *a strong emotional component*. Fight fire with fire. The drive to keep the scruples is essentially emotional: fear. The reasons for change need to have an equally compelling emotional pull. On the grid note the strong *feelings* associated with the reasons. For example, the feeling generated by the look on your child's face when you have to repeat or check something. How

**Figure 5-5**
**Changing Scruples**
**Personal Motivation List**

| Benefits of eliminating scruples | 1. |
| --- | --- |
| | 2. |
| | 3. |
| | 4. |
| | 5. |
| | 6. |
| | 7. |
| | 8. |
| | 9. |
| | 10. |
| Cost of not changing scruples | 1. |
| | 2. |
| | 3. |
| | 4. |
| | 5. |
| | 6. |
| | 7. |
| | 8. |
| | 9. |
| | 10. |

**Figure 5-6**
**Changing Scruples**
**Personal Motivation List**

| Benefits of eliminating scruples | 1. More time for family and fun.<br><br>2. Kids will enjoy me more.<br><br>3. I will feel less anxious.<br><br>4. I can attend worship again.<br><br>5. I will be at peace with God.<br><br>6.<br><br>7.<br><br>8.<br><br>9.<br><br>10. |
|---|---|
| Cost of not changing scruples | 1. Strange looks from loved ones.<br><br>2. I embarrass my family.<br><br>3. Very restricted activities.<br><br>4. Waste a lot of time.<br><br>5. Always making excuses to others.<br><br>6. People avoid me.<br><br>7.<br><br>8.<br><br>9.<br><br>10. |

you felt keeping everybody waiting in the car on the humid summer day while making prolonged safety checks in the house. The feeling that overcame you when you bothered your minister the third time that week to obtain reassurance that you did not sin.

The emphasis on feeling needs to be quite intentional. Logic alone has little impact on fear. Consider how few people abandon prejudice through rational discussion.[7] Prejudice loses its fear component only when people live together and associate with members of the feared group with some degree of equality. *Experience* changes both the feeling *and* the attitude. In gathering motivation, therefore, the person needs to emphasize the emotional aspects as much as possible.

Once the list is complete the person reflects upon it, adding reasons for change and the costs of not changing as they emerge. This process needs to continue until the person makes a firm decision to work on changing scruples. This list should be made as well by people who believe they *already* have made the decision to change. They need to keep the list available so that, if they feel discouraged during the change process, they can review it once again to reduce their ambivalence for change. Motivation to change is not a once-and-for-all event. With ingrained behavior we need to renew our motivation at various stages during our action plan.

## Taking Stock: Preparing for Change

At this point we should take stock and review what is necessary for the next stage. The following components should now be available for the change process.

1) A detailed list of the person's *major obsessions*. (Daily Record of Obsessions and Compulsions)

2) A detailed list of the person's *major compulsions*. (Daily Record of Obsessions and Compulsions)

3) An understanding of the *circumstances* triggering the obsessions and compulsions. (Daily Record of Obsessions and Compulsions)

4) Ratings of the *intensity of the anxiety* triggered by each of the obsessions and compulsions. (Target Obsessions List, Target Compulsions List)

5) A detailed description of the *costs and aggravation* of the scruples. (Personal Motivation List)

6) A detailed description of the *benefits and advantages* of eliminating the scruples.

The reader will find a condensed version of these strategies in Appendix A. Now, with this information the person is ready to move on to the actual change strategies themselves described in the next two chapters.

*Chapter 6*

# Reducing Obsessional Scruples

## Overview of Change Strategy

Before beginning the change strategy itself, the reader may benefit from an explanation of the rationale for the methods described. Keep in mind that we are using a *technique* that works with symptoms of obsessive-compulsive behavior developed by practical and scientifically-minded therapists. In clinical work we frequently use effective treatment methods without fully understanding why or how they work. A good example of this is the use of aspirin in medicine, which decades after its discovery remains mysterious concerning how it works. The explanation for the effectiveness of the change methods for scruples represents science's "best guess," and is not meant to be exhaustive.

Among all the emotional disorders we probably know as much or more about anxiety conditions than all others. Several reasons contribute to this condition. Many aspects of fear are readily observable, and therefore measurable. Treatment success or failure is obvious and we can adjust it accordingly. Successful treatment for fear of flying means that at a minimum the person actually flies in an airplane.

Second, some fears are highly specific. A person with a snake phobia or spider phobia but without other fears or problems provides an excellent chance to study the mechanics of fear reduction. We have learned a great deal about fear reduction from people with specific fears who volunteer for treatment research. Third, fear is also readily observable in animals. Many of the principles of fear reduction were first studied and applied in the laboratory to eliminate "anxiety" or fear in animals. These studies provided therapists with a number of hunches about fear reduction that paid off in clinical work with humans.

*The Exposure Principle.* At the risk of oversimplification, the principle which seems to account for successful elimination of fear and anxiety is *repeated exposure to the feared object or condition.* We will call this principle "exposure" throughout the rest of the book. Freud himself agrees with this principle even though he understood the ultimate explanation of specific fears to have symbolic meaning. For example, he maintained that a fear of knives or sharp objects could represent an underlying fear of castration. Nevertheless, he commented that to eliminate fear, the person had to contact the frightening situation.

Some readers may not care *how* exposure works, only *that* it works. But others might welcome a brief explanation to justify the effort put into the process. When we feel afraid the body releases chemicals triggered by the nervous system. These chemical messages, in turn, activate physical responses which prepare us to take quick action.

A few of these responses include increased heart rate and breathing. Our blood flows from surface areas on our body to muscle areas so we have strength to run away or fight. The pupils of our eyes widen so that we can focus on danger. We all can easily recognize these responses from our own fear experiences. As long as we are in danger the nervous system continues to respond.

What is less obvious to us is that *from the very start of the fear response* the body actually starts a counter-response meant to *return the body to normal activity levels*. With a moment of thought the reason is clear. If fear continued indefinitely, the wear and tear on body tissue would eventually destroy it. Indeed, research now suggests that stress can actually reduce our immune system's ability to fight disease.[1] Our body, then, even in the midst of terror, releases a host of natural calming agents, a series of internal tranquilizers, whose role is to soothe and relax.[2]

The person need not do anything to activate this response since it occurs automatically. However, *as long as danger is perceived*, the fear response will triumph over the calming response. Once the person starts to see that danger no longer exists, this natural calming will triumph.

The second principle which leads to fear reduction and recovery is that our bodies are so constructed that continuous negative stimulation *eventually loses its power to set off a physical reaction*. It is as if the nervous system gets bored with the danger and returns to normal. Scientists call this process of nervous system boredom in the face of threat *habituation*.[3]

Sudden, loud noise provides a good example of this law. Imagine that some type of heavy roadwork machinery starts up outside your window, e.g. a jackhammer breaking up the asphalt road. Your first response is a notable startle. For a few moments the noise is almost deafening. Eventually, you go about your business almost as if the noise is not there, for now it has become part of the background. How could a noise loud enough to startle now have no impact? Our nervous system is constructed to detect changes in the environment, so that we can rapidly respond to sudden danger. However, it "tunes out" or mutes ongoing stimulation.

This same principle works with fear or any other nervous system response. Forcing ourselves to remain in the fear-provoking situation leads gradually to the elimination of intense physical manifestations of fear. Therapists call this process of placing oneself in a fear-provoking situation *exposure*. Exposure is at the heart of fear reduction strategies that lead to habituation.[4] Exposure represents exactly one-half of the effective treatment for scruples and OCD.

Successful exposure has several qualities. First, exposure must be *prolonged*. The exact amount of time is unknown, but we know that exposure will not work if it is brief or fleeting. Second, the person must *experience some level of anxiety* during the exposure. This notion may scare off a person with scruples or other fears. But before anyone gives up at this point, all the principle says is that exposure involves *some* anxiety. It does not require *maximum* fear. Teaching someone who is afraid of water to swim does not call for throwing him or her into the deep end of the pool. Rather, gradual exposure in the shallow end where swimming techniques are safely learned will work, even though the swimmer will experience some anxiety even there. The same principle works for exposure therapy. The trick, as we shall see below, is discovering what constitutes the equivalent of the shallow end of the pool for each fear tackled.

The second principle means, therefore, that the person needs to focus on the fearful event. Total distraction through mental activity or the use of alcohol or drugs does not allow the nervous system to learn that no true danger exists. Distraction will allow the person to cope momentarily with the fear situation, and that may at times be the best one can do. However, distraction does not lead to permanent fear reduction.

Third, exposure needs to be *repeated*. One experience is insufficient. Focusing on the baby's breathing in the middle of the night may need to reoccur for permanent relief. Again, we cannot prescribe the precise number of exposure events required. Indeed, the first few exposure sessions may actually increase fear since the person has avoided the situation or not thought about it for a long time. But because the session is prolonged, anxiety gradually decreases.

Fourth, exposure may take place in *the real situation or through imagination*. Some fears occur in places that are practical for planning exposure sessions. For example, if praying in the church or synagogue triggers blasphemous thoughts, creating an exposure session is easy to arrange. Other situations are more difficult to arrange, e.g. fears related to sexual performance. In these cases exposure can take place in imagination. As a rule-of-thumb, however, live exposure is much more efficient than imaginal exposure, and should take priority.

*The Blocking Principle.* With OCD and scruples, therapists discovered that they had to add another twist to exposure strategies to eliminate symptoms completely. If we give the problem a moment's thought the reason is evident. Recall from our description in Chapter 2 that obsessions and compulsions have different functions. Obsessions (recurrent unwanted thoughts, images, urges, acts) *trigger* anxiety. Compulsions (recurrent unwanted acts, thoughts, images, urges) *relieve* anxiety. If each time an obsession occurs the person performs some compulsion to relieve the anxiety, no new learning takes place.

When a parent checks a sleeping baby again and again, learning to live without total certainty never takes place.[5] Let us imagine what would happen in this case with exposure alone. If the parent listens to the baby's breathing from another room, anxiety will increase. Each time the parent checks on the baby, anxiety momentarily decreases. Since checking turns off the anxiety the parent keeps checking. The fear *does not remain long enough to allow the remedy of nervous system boredom (habituation) to set in.*

Reducing anxiety and fear with scruples, therefore, requires a second component; *the blocking principle.*[6] The blocking principle requires the person to *block the compulsion itself*, whether it is a physical or mental act. If the compulsion does not turn off the anxiety, exposure has a chance to work. Changing scruples and OCD symptoms, therefore, is a two-step process: exposure to the obsessions, and, *at the same time*, blocking the compulsions.

In Chapter 4 we discussed pastoral care strategies that went back centuries in the church. We can now review some of those components to see how they dovetail with the principles of behavioral psychology.

According to church rules, the scrupulous person has a *duty* to act contrary to the scruples to avoid psychological and moral paralysis. This obviously provides a motivational component that involves both exposure and blocking. Second, one can use the behavior of conscientious persons as models. This is a modeling component, which eliminates the doubting component through externally-generated standards of conduct. Third, one should follow the guidance of a single spiritual or moral authority faithfully. This provides an educative component which, again, helps generate alternative standards of conduct from internal scrupulous ones. Fourth, one may and should place oneself directly in situations or circumstances which trigger the scruples. One could hardly generate a better definition of the exposure principle. Finally, one should not repeat religious rituals. Again, this is an excellent definition of blocking the compulsion.

We use these ancient principles to remind those desiring to change scrupulous behavior that the insights of modern behavioral psychology are only a more systematic elaboration of the collective wisdom of centuries of pastoral practice.

*Employing a Helper.* A supportive friend, spouse, or relative enhances the efficiency and effectiveness of the change strategies. Although many persons with scruples might feel hesitant to solicit help, a trustworthy companion far outweighs any momentary embarrassment.

A helper plays several important roles. We know that engaging others is an effective motivator for change. When going on a diet or planning an exercise program, the best strategy is to tell the world. Public commitment serves as an excellent self-reminder. Helpers also provide moral support, which is especially useful when anxiety starts to rise slightly during the initial exposure sessions. Perhaps most importantly, the helper assists the person with the blocking principle—ensuring that the individual does not go back to check how a task was done or seek reassurance.[7]

The helper needs to remain task-oriented and unemotional if the partner hesitates or becomes upset. Under no circumstances should the helper use anger, ridicule, or sarcasm as motivators.[8] Humor can be especially effective for bonding and helping the person gain perspective about the symptoms. But humor must be viewed as laughing-with, not laughing-at, the person.

In the remaining sections of this chapter we focus primarily on the first part of the obsessional-compulsive link: planning and carrying out the exposure component. But this represents only one of two essential

ingredients. Exposure alone will work only if the person has no neutralizing compulsion. Obsessions that exist in conjunction with compulsions require the blocking strategy as well.

### Obsessions: Change Strategies

With the exception of obsessional scruples that have no compulsions, changing obsessions must occur *simultaneously* with changing
compulsions. To simplify the explanation of change strategies, however, we need to discuss them separately.

*Identify Target Obsessions.* The person needs to examine the list of
obsessions generated during the assessment phase (see Chapter 5). The
person, perhaps in conjunction with a counselor, simplifies the list into
a final target list of obsessional scruples to change (Figure 6-1). Select
first an obsession which triggers *a lower level of anxiety.* Fear reduction is like climbing a ladder; wisdom suggests starting with the lowest
step first. People are more likely to try the strategy if the fear is manageable at first, and success in one area will encourage the person to
take bigger steps later. Target the obsession that triggers, on average,
the least amount of tension.

*Break Down Target Obsessions into Small Steps for Imagination
Exposure.* Some obsessions, as noted above, realistically can occur
only in imagination. Although a person can place himself in situations
likely to trigger an obsession, the exact obsession cannot, and often
should not, happen in real life. An example of this type of obsession is
worries about injury or safety. Exposure in these cases must happen in
imagination. The person needs to develop scenes or imaginary pictures
about the obsession to think about.

For the same reason that we choose a low-level obsession first, break
down the target obsessions into small steps for greater success. Figure
6-2, the Target Symptoms List from the Yale–Brown Obsessive-
Compulsive Scale is handy for breaking down target obsessions into
small steps. If a mother obsesses about her child's safety, she can break
it down from less to more serious concerns—for example: minor hurts
(bruise on the knee), minor illness (cold), minor absences (five minutes
later than expected), all the way up to more serious mishaps (e.g.
breaks leg playing soccer, becomes unconscious in a traffic accident).

Make a list of approximately ten situations going from least to most
anxiety provoking for each separate obsessional theme. Since this is not
an exact science, be prepared to add or discard themes as needed.

**Figure 6-1**
**Target Obsessions List**

---

**OBSESSION:** Thought, image, impulse or behavior that *triggers* anxiety.

|  | Average Tension Level |
|---|---|
| 1. Angry with spouse; God will punish me | 7 |
| 2. Store clerk returned too much change | 8 |
| 3. "Love of neighbor" means greeting everyone | 5 |
| 4. Idea to hit people when I cross a busy street | 7 |
| 5. Urge/idea to make obscene phone call | 9 |
| 6. Idea of running people down with my car | 8 |
| 7. Thought that God is really the Evil One | 10 |
| 8. Playing with my child may physically injure her | 6 |
| 9. | |
| 10. | |

**Tension Level**

| 1 | = No anxiety |
|---|---|
| 2-3 | = Mild anxiety |
| 4-5 | = Moderate anxiety |
| 6-7 | = Severe anxiety |
| 8-10 | = Intense anxiety |

**Guidelines:**
Work first on obsession that generates *least* amount of tension, on average. (Do not obsess if some are very close. Pick any one, flip a coin, etc.)

From: Joseph W. Ciarrocchi, Ph.D.
  *The Doubting Disease*
  Paulist Press

Copy worksheet for personal or therapeutic use.

---

*Identify Exposure Situations.* Other obsessions are readily triggered by real life exposure. Walking into a place of worship, for example, may immediately trigger blasphemous thoughts. Looking at an attractive person generates an immediate doubt that one has sinned. Calculating semester grades makes a teacher believe he or she has made a mistake. Looking at a sleeping baby triggers violent thoughts. These obsessions lend themselves to real-life exposure, which is quite efficient in fear reduction.

The basic principle is to identify situations which will *provoke* the obsession, i.e. cause it to happen. Change cannot occur if the obsession is not even present. Make a list of potential exposure situations using the Target Symptoms List (Figure 6-2). As in the case of imaginal exposure described in the previous section, break down the situations triggering obsessions according to the amount of anxiety each generates. Using the 1-10 tension-level scale, rank each item according to the anxiety generated. Once again, you will choose situations at the lower end of the scale to change first.

*Give Yourself Permission To Enact the Exposure Strategy.* This item separates out people with scruples from those with non-religious obsessions and compulsions. If the treatment of scruples differs in any significant way from that of OCD in general, it results from people believing that *the therapy tasks themselves may in some way be wrong from a moral or religious standpoint.*

Let us take the example of a man who believes that to experience delight when looking at an attractive woman means that he is risking the sin of "having already committed adultery with her in his heart" (Matthew 5:27-28). An exposure task might include visiting a busy indoor shopping mall, sitting down with a drink, and looking in a natural way at passers-by, both men and women. The person immediately objects, "I am risking sin by doing this." How can this doubt be resolved? If the person with scruples could easily resolve the doubt, by definition he or she would not be bothered by scruples. Yet, failure to use exposure means that the fear will remain. If the person is in therapy, this issue may trigger conflict with the therapist. The therapist, for her part, may not understand the client's "resistance" to a seemingly simple exercise. The client, for his part, is unwilling to entrust the state of his immortal soul to another person, particularly if he does not view the therapist as a religious expert.

Many people with scruples get stuck on this point. With my own

**Figure 6-2**
**Target Symptoms List**

---

PATIENT NAME _____ Mary _____ DATE 9/10

**OBSESSIONS**

   TARGET - 1 <u>Worry about child's safety; minor hurts, bruise on knee.</u>

   TARGET - 2 <u>Minor absence: Five minutes late getting home.</u>

   TARGET - 3 <u>Twists her ankle.</u>

   TARGET - 4 <u>Breaks her leg.</u>

**COMPULSIONS**

   TARGET - 1 _____

   TARGET - 2 _____

   TARGET - 3 _____

   TARGET - 4 _____

**AVOIDANCE**

---

From: Yale-Brown Obsessive-Compulsive Scale. Reprinted with permission.

clients I sometimes share my background in theology, and this some-times, but not always, helps them trust the exposure process. I have learned that referral to and collaboration with a religious professional is effective. Psychiatrist David Greenberg suggests how to structure this collaboration.[9] If someone is hesitant about the ethical legitimacy of exposure tasks, he or she should take the list of tasks to a spiritual or religious consultant of the person's choosing. The consultant is asked the following question about each of the tasks: "Is it permitted for me to...?" Then the consultant discusses *each* item with the person, keep-ing the permissible ones. A creative therapist can almost always gener-ate permissible tasks with a client if done in this collaborative manner. (We will repeat this same recommendation when discussing the block-ing strategies, so for the sake of efficiency the person would want to seek permission when *both* lists are ready.)

This method relieves the counselor from struggling with the client about compliance with the strategy from a religious viewpoint. Instead the counselor can attend to the technical demands of the change process itself, and feel assured the client's values were respected. The client can now more freely engage (cognitively) in the change process, and be reminded that no moral justification exists for not participating.

*Carry Out the Exposure.* Plan sufficient time to carry out exposure sessions. Anywhere from 30 to 90 minutes may be necessary for a ses-sion. Select the obsession with the least anxiety. Select, if available, one that allows "live" exposure rather than in imagination.

Start with the situation from the target obsessions sub-goals list that generates the least tension. Let yourself feel the fear. Write down the intensity of the fear (on a scale of 1-10) when you start and again when you finish. (See Figures 6-3 and 6-4 for a worksheet and example for changing obsessions.) The next chapter will discuss how you need to block the compulsions/rituals *at the same time.* If no compulsion exists for this particular obsession, simply feel the fear.

Allow enough time for the fear to surface and then decline. This may take anywhere from 30 to 90 minutes. For example, looking at a reli-gious symbol or statue might trigger blasphemous thoughts. For other situations exposure might be relatively brief. For example, the urge to undress in church may happen only when first going in. The person could enter, remain until the urge passes, and repeat the exposure a few times until little anxiety remains upon entering. In treating a minister who had obsessions when looking at medical paraphernalia, we loaned

**Figure 6-3**
**Worksheet for Changing Obsessions**

**Day/Date**

| Obsession: | Exposure Strategy: | | | Guidelines: |
|---|---|---|---|---|
| Disturbing thought, doubt, activity, or impulse that *triggers* anxiety. | 1) Spend 15-90 minutes staying in situation that triggers obsession. OR 2) Intentionally provoke the obsession and dwell on it for 15-90 minutes. | | | 1) Stay in situation or think about obsession until tension level drops to mild range. Scale 1 = No anxiety 2-3 = Mild anxiety 4-5 = Moderate anxiety 6-7 = Severe anxiety 8-10 = Intense anxiety |
| | Initial Tension Level 1-10 | Amount of time spent exposed to obsession | Final Tension Level 1-10 | 2) If anxiety becomes intense consider "reporter" strategy while dwelling on obsession. |

Joseph W. Ciarrocchi, Ph.D.
*The Doubting Disease*
Paulist Press

Copy worksheet for personal or therapeutic use.

**Figure 6-4**
**Worksheet for Changing Obsessions**

Day/Date

| Obsession: | | Exposure Strategy: | | | Guidelines: |
|---|---|---|---|---|---|
| Disturbing thought, doubt, activity, or impulse that *triggers* anxiety. | | 1) Spend 15-90 minutes staying in situation that triggers obsession. OR 2) Intentionally provoke the obsession and dwell on it for 15-90 minutes. | | | 1) Stay in situation or think about obsession until tension level drops to mild range. |
| | | Initial Tension Level 1-10 (7) | Amount of time spent exposed to obsession | Final Tension Level 1-10 (3) | Scale 1 = No anxiety 2-3 = Mild anxiety 4-5 = Moderate anxiety 6-7 = Severe anxiety 8-10 = Intense anxiety |
| Spouse forgot my birthday. I got angry, then worried he would die in an accident as God's punishment to me. | | For 30 minutes I thought about him being killed or injured. | | | 2) If anxiety becomes intense consider "reporter" strategy while dwelling on obsession. I tried to focus on the physical details of the scenes. |

From:    Joseph W. Ciarrocchi, Ph.D.          Copy worksheet for personal
         *The Doubting Disease*                   or therapeutic use.
         Paulist Press

him plastic syringes, tape, bandages and other items from our clinic. He was told to take out the bag of items for prolonged sessions several times a week. In another instance a church worker obsessed about little white specks on the carpet and would not vacuum because they might be remnants from holy communion. He was instructed to place tiny pieces of paper all over the rug and then vacuum. Another person believed that candy sent to her for a holiday was somehow contaminated. She was instructed to leave it opened for sharing in the faculty room (after her therapist first sampled the coconut creams).

After exposure has reduced anxiety for one target obsession into the mild range, move on to the next more difficult one. Gradually, all obsessions for which exposure can be carried out in external situations are eliminated or reduced to manageable anxiety levels.

Obsessions which need to take place in imagination require a different approach. The person first identifies the theme at work from the Target Obsessions List. It should be one that triggers the least, or minimal, level of anxiety. As suggested above, the theme should be broken down into a list of smaller, more manageable steps in the obsession (again, the Target Obsessions List). Recall the example of worry about loved ones dying in a car crash.

Set aside one to two hours to work on exposure in imagination. Begin with the scene from one theme which is least upsetting. Record anxiety at the start of imagining the scene. Imagine the scene as vividly as possible, for as long as possible. Stay with the scene until the anxiety remains in the mild range after several trials.

Some people have trouble imagining scenes, or staying with the scene in their minds. Therapists Gail Steketee and Kerrin White have several recommendations if this happens.[10] 1) Put the scene on an audio tape, so that it repeats over and over. Your own voice may work, or the voice of a friend or relative may make it more vivid. 2) Focus on different parts of the scene: what is the person *feeling*, what is the person *thinking*, what are the *sensory* experiences (feel, touch, taste, smell, etc.)? A hospital chaplaincy trainee was injury-phobic and could not listen to people describing their physical ailments, particularly if they described surgery or broken bones. His friend, who recently broke his arm, described the entire ordeal on tape including the accident, the visit to the emergency room, the orthopedist needing to rebreak the bone to reset it, and subsequent follow-up visits. The trainee repeatedly listened to the tape until the description no longer upset him.

When all scenes for one theme are complete, move on to the next theme by degree of difficulty. Follow the same procedure until anxiety is reduced for all. If motivation suffers during this experience, the person should review the Personal Motivation List constructed in the last chapter (see also Appendix A). This review, in conjunction with success in reducing anxiety, should generate even greater courage in attacking the remaining, more powerful obsessions.

Once exposure to the original list of target obsessions is complete, take stock of how complete the change is. It is common to remember or become aware of major obsessions and compulsions while doing the actual exposure. This is no cause for alarm. Rather, simply add this to the Target Obsessions List and tackle it in the same way as the other obsessions. The exact amount of exposure required varies from person to person and degree of fear. Experienced clinicians indicate that a total of about 20 hours of exposure for all symptoms over a course of several weeks or months is effective in most instances.[11]

"Success" in treatment of scruples is not an all-or-none cure in the traditional sense. People with scruples are prone to dwell on doubts and worries. Rather, success involves having an effective coping strategy for any old or new obsession that arises. We will discuss this issue more fully when we suggest maintenance strategies for long-term care.

We now turn our attention to the second major component of the change strategy: blocking the compulsions (response prevention).

*Chapter 7*

# Reducing Compulsive Scruples

## Overview of Change Strategy

We cannot emphasize enough that, in most cases, reducing scruples is a two-part process which the person carries out simultaneously. No change in rituals will occur if one exposes oneself to the obsessional scruple, but continues to perform the ritual. People must experience the fear, and, at the same time, block or prevent the ritual/compulsion.

The exception to this is when ritual behavior occurs without an obsession preceding it. For example, someone repeats prayers seven times because doing that particular number is somehow comforting. The origin of this relief may be lost to the person's memory. So the ritual occurs whenever the person prays, not in response to a particular thought, image, or urge. This leads, then, to a practical rule. If there are no rituals (either external or mental), exposure to the obsession is sufficient. If there is no triggering obsession (external or mental), blocking the ritual in the situation is sufficient.

In this section we will describe the method for blocking rituals in its application to compulsive scruples. By now the reader can predict that the first stage is targeting the rituals for change. Again, we recommend that the person develop this list from the self-monitoring phase of the change program (see Chapter 5). From this information the person constructs a list of rituals, again noting the anxiety associated with their non-performance (Target Compulsions List, Figure 7-1). That is, how anxious does the person feel if the ritual is not carried out?

Choosing where to start is partially determined by the obsession list. The person both exposes to a lesser anxiety-producing obsession *and* blocks the ritual. Note carefully the particular obsession that goes with each ritual. This will ensure that each ritual has a corresponding obsession and vice versa. If there are only rituals, then the person can start with any low or mild anxiety-producing one on the list.

**Figure 7-1**
**Target Compulsions List**

---

**COMPULSIONS:** Thought, image, impulse or behavior that
*reduces* anxiety.

|  | Average Tension Level |
|---|---|
| 1. Praying for spouse so that he or she doesn't die | 7 |
| 2. Checking grocery receipts for mistakes | 8 |
| 3. Greeting everyone "hello" as sign of charity | 5 |
| 4. Hold package in hands to prevent hitting anyone | 7 |
| 5. Cover telephone to prevent obscene phone call | 9 |
| 6. Drive slowly to not hit people | 8 |
| 7. Long prayers at thought, "God is Evil" | 10 |
| 8. Check child's condition repeatedly when playing | 6 |
| 9. | |
| 10. | |

**Tension Level**
1     = No anxiety
2-3   = Mild anxiety
4-5   = Moderate anxiety
6-7   = Severe anxiety
8-10  = Intense anxiety

**Guidelines:**
Work first on compulsion that triggers *least* amount of tension, on average. (Do not obsess if some are very close.)

From: Joseph W. Ciarrocchi, Ph.D.
     *The Doubting Disease*
     Paulist Press

Copy worksheet for personal or therapeutic use.

---

Again, the method requires distinguishing *external* rituals from *purely mental* ones. External rituals are easier to monitor. An observer could verify whether or not the ritual took place. Mental or cognitive rituals take place within the person's mind, and are known only to the person. To block mental rituals, which are often automatic, requires developing self-observation and mental control to a high degree. Recall John Bunyan's obsession with the thought, "Sell Christ, sell Him, sell Him." Consider the difficulty of blocking his mental ritual which was saying "Never, never" each time the thought arose. Yet this precisely is what the strategy involves. For this reason, I usually suggest starting with external rituals if they exist.

Now the two strategies of exposure and blocking come together. Exposure to the obsession takes place along with blocking the ritual. For a full understanding of blocking rituals we need to recall a distinction made earlier about two types of rituals: positive and avoidance ones. Positive rituals are meant to neutralize or *undo the anxiety* generated by some behavior—for example, saying a prayer after blasphemous thoughts, as did Bunyan. Avoidance rituals are a means of *self-control* to *prevent some undesired behavior*—for example, the person who carried bags in both hands when crossing an intersection to avoid punching people.

Blocking, then, might mean one of two possible responses. It might mean *not doing an act* (e.g. saying a prayer) with a positive ritual. Or it might mean *doing an act* (such as crossing the streets while swinging your arms naturally) with an avoidance ritual.

The person, therefore, needs to determine *what form blocking will take for each target ritual*. I simplified the process for my clients by giving them one single sheet (Figures 7-2 and 7-3) with the instructions "Do the Opposite" of the ritual. St. Ignatius had given the equivalent instruction through the phrase *agere contra* (do the opposite) four centuries ago. This notion of acting against the scruple combines both the exposure and blocking components in one thrust.

The following represent examples of the different forms that blocking (doing the opposite) might take. 1) If sharp objects trigger aggression phobias, leave them out in plain view. 2) If "charity" demands greeting every passer-by on the street, remain silent. 3) If one worries about communion specks on the rug, step purposely on the alleged spots. 4) If thoughts about loved ones dying are followed by prayers for their safety, stop praying. 5) If the channels are changed constantly to

**Figure 7-2**
**Worksheet for Changing Compulsions**

**Day/Date**

| Exposure Strategy: | Compulsion: | Guidelines: |
|---|---|---|
| Think about or place yourself in situations that trigger disturbing thought, impulse, image or ritual. | Thought, image, impulse, or act that *reduces* anxiety. | 1) Stay in situation until tension level drops to mild range. |
| Describe situation or thought. | *Blocking Strategy: Do the Opposite.*<br>1) If impulse to *avoid* object or activity— *DO IT.*<br>2) If impulse to do something: e.g. repeat, check, pray, seek reassurance— *prevent the response.* | Scale<br>1 = No anxiety<br>2-3 = Mild anxiety<br>4-5 = Moderate anxiety<br>6-7 = Severe anxiety<br>8-10 = Intense anxiety |
|  | Initial Tension Level 1-10 | Amount of time spent exposed to situation | Final Tension Level 1-10 | 2) If anxiety becomes intense, consider "reporter" strategy while staying in situation. |

From:   Joseph W. Ciarrocchi, Ph.D.
        *The Doubting Disease*
        Paulist Press

Copy worksheet for personal or therapeutic use.

**Day/Date**

**Figure 7-3**
**Worksheet for Changing Compulsions**

| Exposure Strategy: | Compulsion: | Guidelines |
|---|---|---|
| Think about or place yourself in situations that trigger disturbing thought, impulse, image or ritual. | Thought, image, impulse, or act that *reduces* anxiety.<br><br>*Blocking Strategy: Do the Opposite.*<br>1) If impulse to *avoid* object or activity— *DO IT.*<br>2) If impulse to do something: e.g. repeat, check, pray, seek reassurance— *prevent the response.* | 1) Stay in situation until tension level drops to mild range.<br><br>Scale<br>1   = No anxiety<br>2-3 = Mild anxiety<br>4-5 = Moderate anxiety<br>6-7 = Severe anxiety<br>8-10 = Intense anxiety |
| Describe situation or thought. | Initial Tension Level 1-10 (6)    Amount of time spent exposed to situation    Final Tension Level 1-10 (3) | 2) If anxiety becomes intense, consider "reporter" strategy while staying in situation. |
| Playing "piggyback" or "rough-house" with my two-year old child. | Played for 20 minutes with her, and did not ask her if she was all right. | I tried to listen to her giggling and laughter as a distraction to my anxiety. |

From: Joseph W. Ciarrocchi, Ph.D.- *The Doubting Disease* - Paulist Press — Copy worksheet for personal or therapeutic use avoid seeing shows that might trigger sexual thoughts, watch an entire show with commercials straight through. 6) If apologies are frequent to people for alleged "wrongs," do not apologize. 7) If religious professionals need to give frequent reassurance, act without consultation. 8) If blasphemous thoughts are followed by "corrective" prayers, let the thoughts come and do not pray in response to them. 9) If sexual thoughts about one's child cause avoidance of normal hygiene duties, then perform washing, diapering, bathing, etc., as often as caretakers normally do. 10) If I avoid hugging a friend or child of the same sex for fear of being homosexual, find reasonable opportunities to hug them.

### Guidelines for Blocking

*Give Yourself Permission To "Do the Opposite."* As in the case of exposure strategies, the person might benefit from taking the Target Compulsions List to a spiritual or religious consultant. Describe the purpose of doing the opposite and ask if the blocking strategies are permitted in each case. Keep those that are permitted, and obtain alternative suggestions for those which are not. If the person is comfortable with the list as is, then one can begin without this consultation.

*Determining What's Normal.* What is "normal" for a person's culture regarding social courtesies, cleaning babies, taking a bath, watching television shows, leaving out sharp objects, etc.? Positive rituals are often exaggerations of adaptive behavior such as grooming, gathering, and checking. With scruples and OCD, however, the person seems to lack the "off" switch that others have to determine when "enough's enough."

If in doubt, the person can use the tradition of moral theology we cited in Chapter 4. The medieval theologian Thomas Aquinas (hardly a libertine) advised that in unclear ethical situations the person should follow the behavior of the so-called "prudent" person. Prudent people can help set guidelines for the scrupulous, and may include a religious guide or any person that strikes one as having common sense. Behavior therapy refers to this strategy as modeling.

*Putting It All Together.* Armed with the stepladder list of obsessions combined with specific blocking guidelines, the person is now ready to carry out the entire change strategy. Beginning with lower level examples of obsessions, the person uses exposure to trigger the obsession and does the opposite of the ritual impulse. As noted above, the person stays in the situation, either for real or in imagination, long enough to experience the anxiety and watch it decline. This usually requires 30 to 90 minutes.

After the person experiences success with one item on the list, the next one is tackled. For example, a mother listens to an audiotape describing her child bruising a knee, and at the same time prevents praying as a response. She listens to this tape repeatedly until the urge to ritualize is reduced as well as the fear from the scene itself. Then she might listen next to a description of the child falling on her knee and cutting it.

Reducing fear and the urge to ritualize is not the same as *feeling good* about the scene. Most obsessional scenes are about real life horrors. No one enjoys thinking these thoughts. Reducing the fear and disgust means reducing the urge to ritualize as the way to escape these thoughts or impulses.

*Getting Stuck.* If repeated attempts at exposure are not successful in eliminating fear or result in continuing to ritualize, a change in scene or situation is required. The person needs to rearrange the scene or situation to a less threatening one with similar content. Thinking about my child breaking a leg might be too difficult. Try shifting to a scene which involves a lesser injury, e.g. sprains an ankle. If looking at romantic scenes on television is overwhelming, perhaps just listening to the dialogue at first will work.

## Accepting the Unacceptable

The core conflict in scruples and OCD is the notion that the idea, image, or impulse is dangerous or unacceptable. As we noted in the section on mental suppression, running away only makes them more vivid and frequent. Clients are often shocked when I suggest that they need to accept their impulses. Often the impulses are repulsive, disgusting and immoral. One does not have to *like* or *enjoy* the impulses; one has to accept their existence calmly. A matter-of-fact acceptance is the equivalent of exposing the self to the feared event, and gaining mastery by exposure.

The strategies recommended up to this point involve exposure in the real or imagined situation to the obsession, while at the same time blocking any ritual. The strategy described next is a purely cognitive one which also has the effect of facing the obsession (exposure). However, the person tries to manage the anxiety through focused attentional strategies. Although we have no direct empirical support for the effectiveness of this strategy for OCD specifically, several studies have shown that treatment packages using the strategy improve emotion regulation for depressed and abused patients.[1]

I have dubbed this method the "reporter strategy." When experiencing an unacceptable feeling, idea, image or impulse, the person attempts to confront the event as would a reporter. That is, one tries to describe the experience neutrally, in descriptive language, and *never evaluate or judge the event*. One client told me after using the strategy that "it takes the edge off the obsession." This exposure reduces the power of the obsession, and the person is able to use other adaptive measures to remain functional.

Learning the reporter strategy proceeds in two stages. First, use the strategy for a non-OCD event to develop a sense of the technique. Below are examples of using it for an everyday event.

> *Lacing and tying shoes.* I see two brown shoes on the floor, and I reach first for the left one. I slowly loosen the laces, and notice that the ends of each lace are slightly frayed. The brown of the lace is slightly darker than the tone of the shoe itself. The heel is worn considerably, and the front and back have notable scuff marks that are a much lighter color than the non-scuffed sections. The shoe slips comfortably over my foot, and then I feel a sharp, tiny pain at the toe. I remove the shoe and shake out a small pebble caught from a walk in the park yesterday. The shoe goes back on, this time with no obstruction. I take the lace in my right hand and lace first one side, then the next, up to the top eyelet. I pull tightly on the laces, one end in each hand until I feel considerable pressure on my instep, etc.

Other examples might include taking a bath, shampooing, walking in the park, swimming, riding a bike, or washing dishes. The key ingredients include observing, describing, and not judging. In the example above, notice that the reporter does not say, "It's just awful that this stone is in my shoe." Rather, the observation is limited to the experience of pain and then a description of its cause (the pebble). Evaluative comments are kept out as much as possible. Description is the correct path. A better statement than "The spray of the water on my back is the best thing that happened to me all day" would be, "The water loosens and soothes my neck muscles and skin."

Once a person feels comfortable using the strategy for non-OCD events, he or she moves on to an obsessional experience. The same strategy applies. The person observes, describes, but does not judge the self for any aspect: not the image, idea, urge or impulse, nor any of the feelings or behavioral tendencies that result from the obsession. Below is an example of someone having a personally unacceptable obsession with a sexual content.

> *Reporter Strategy with a Sexual Obsession.* (When driving a car down a city street, the person catches a glimpse of possibly the most physically attractive person he or she has ever seen. The heat of the attraction is immediately followed by the obsession that one may be sinning unless the image is rejected. This immediately generates an obsession that perhaps one is dwelling on "bad thoughts," or just about to dwell on them. The reporter strategy suggests dealing with such an image or idea in the following way.)

> The person was walking under a street lamp at a fairly brisk pace. I caught a glimpse of flowing dark hair caught up in the breeze. The person was dressed in tennis shoes, two-tone, I think, with no socks. The color of the jeans was dark black with a designer label on the right back pocket. Several people parted on the sidewalk when the person passed, and they glanced back over their shoulders with a notable double-take of their heads. The person's collar was turned up slightly around the neck. The figure passed too quickly to see much of the face, but the shape was slim and contoured. I noticed that my hands were gripping the steering wheel tightly and that my heartbeat had increased, and my breathing rate felt quicker. My mind continues to focus back on the image of the person passing. The person was walking under a street lamp at a fairly brisk pace. I caught a glimpse of flowing dark hair.... (Continue to repeat the scenario as described, over and over.)

Sometimes confusion occurs over this strategy. Some ask, "But isn't this 'entertaining' the bad thought, and likely to increase the sexual attraction?" As my client reported above, it actually takes the edge off the obsession. By not trying to suppress the image, it lessens the likelihood that the image will continue to rebound and haunt us as happens with the "white bear" phenomenon. Also, the person is *not* emphasizing the sexual components of the event, but puts the entire event in a descriptive, material context. Far from focusing on the sexual meaning of the event, this strategy defuses the electricity of its titillating features. The image becomes prosaic and asexual.

Again, for the strategy to work, the description must be non-judgmental. The description should sound like the opening lines of a news story. Ideas or descriptors such as "I must be perverted" have to be replaced with the objective language of the scenario above.[2]

*Summary.* The last three chapters form the heart of change strategies for scruples. A reader may feel overwhelmed by the various twists and turns taken in the change description. Although everyone does not need to know some of the scientific or historical background interwoven in the book, I find that many clients appreciate this information. My experience confirms that people with OCD and scruples are skilled abstract thinkers and often request detailed explanations. The danger is that the reader may lose the forest for the trees.

This last effect would be a sad one, since, despite the clinical skills required to deal with difficult cases, the process of fear reduction has a simple elegance to it. Getting stuck should only suggest that a person may need some assistance in carrying out the strategies, rather than abandoning them.

To prevent missing the forest for the trees, I have condensed these last three chapters in Appendix A along with the relevant record sheets. After reading the detailed explanations in context, the reader should have the capacity to use Appendix A effectively. I have also provided Appendix B for the Obsessions and Compulsions Checklist from the Yale-Brown Obsessive-Compulsive Scale for self-assessment of OCD symptoms.

## Living with Scrupulous Persons

Not only are scruples a painful personal experience, but they usually create tension for family members and companions. In the least observable form, the person suffers privately with mental obsessions and compulsions, but the preoccupation and depression render him or her unavailable to friends or family. They may notice increased irritability or a desire to be left alone.

External compulsions are likely to have the most disruptive impact on family life. The degree of disruption depends on the compulsion itself, and varies from the mildly annoying to extreme aggravation. Checking for safety may disrupt daily living. Safety concerns about children may result in overprotection and keep them from experiencing normal social activities (school trips, visits to friends, riding in other people's cars, etc.). Rituals which consume time may bring family life to a standstill or require accommodation. These include such items as multiple washing of dishes, frequent bathing, excessive praying, repeating religious exercises, constant requests for reassurance, inability to clean certain "off-limits" household areas, or inability to perform hygiene with children for fear of hurting them or having "bad thoughts." It takes little imagination to appreciate how this disrupts family life.

People living with or personally involved with scrupulous persons sometimes request guidelines for supporting them without getting caught up in the problem itself. The first requirement is to educate friends, family members, or employers about scruples and OCD. This can be done through reading (e.g. the annotated references at the end of this book), or consultation with a competent professional. Chapter 8 provides annotated references for the general reader and guidelines for obtaining professional help.

Sometimes persons with OCD or scruples will request that friends and family help with the external compulsions or ritual aspects of the disorder. For example, if a person obsesses that a thought was "uncharitable" he may ask the spouse repeatedly for forgiveness, and will not rest until the words "I forgive you" are spoken. Naturally this becomes tiresome to the "offended" partner, and sometimes only extreme anger will make the person back off from the request. However, this sets up a cycle of using anger or even rage to stop the rituals, and this hurts the relationship. Such faulty interaction patterns sometimes are the motivating force behind seeking treatment for scruples.

Once significant others understand the role of rituals and external compulsions, they are in a position to support treatment. They need to stop assisting the person with rituals, because they inadvertently have become part of the ritual. Recall that compulsions neutralize the anxiety generated by the obsession. Each time the compulsion is carried out it reinforces the behavior because it turns off something painful. If friends or family assist in this "turning-off" sequence, this prevents the person from facing the fear directly and allowing the principle of habituation to work.

The foremost authority on fear reduction, psychiatrist Isaac Marks, advises family members to say kindly, "The doctor said we were not to do that for you," or "The doctor said we are not to tell you that, now."[3] Friends and family must participate in this process *without intense external anger.* They should make these statements calmly and sympathetically, appreciating the pain and turmoil the person experiences when the ritual cannot be carried out. If a person cannot respond calmly, walking away is a better temporary solution than an argument. Gradually the person learns that using others to carry out rituals has come to an end. This will not "cure" the scruples, but at least it makes carrying out the rituals more bothersome, and perhaps this will motivate him or her to follow professional advice. Readers familiar with the problems associated with living with an addicted person will recognize this as overcoming "enabling" behavior.[4]

Somewhat more complicated to handle are system maintenance problems. Some persons with OCD hoard objects, e.g. junk mail, trash, store coupons, worthless newspapers or magazines. Their rationale is usually a vague sense of "someday I may need these things." Fear of contamination may leave the bathroom a disaster area. Cleaning the bathroom or tossing out the collectibles is necessary for sane living. In these instances family members are acting contrary to the compulsion. This will generate anxiety for the person, but the family must take care of its own needs.

Families and friends may obtain more specific guidelines from competent professionals, since the manifestation of obsessions and compulsions varies in unpredictable ways.

## The Agnostic or Unbeliever

Although it may seem paradoxical, agnostics and unbelievers also are prone to scruples. Scruples in the agnostic often resemble scruples in the religious person. The greatest resemblance is in interpersonal moral behavior. For example, the agnostic may worry to the same degree as the religious person about whether or not he or she has caused harm to someone by an action. The major difference is that *ethical, moral and psychological guilt* drive the agnostic, and *religious guilt* burdens the believer as well. From the outside, then, some forms of scruples will look the same in both persons. Each may show excessive concern about physically harming others, or hurting someone's feelings, and require repeated reassurances of approval.

The nature of scruples will sometimes lead the person to seek help from persons with specialized training in ethical theory or even pastoral ministers. Some agnostics were raised in households that lacked religious training, while others have moved away from religious belief during their own life journey. Indeed, a number of persons in this group expressly leave religion because of scruples. They describe similar horror stories to those of the believer with scruples, but at some point decide to bail out of religious practices altogether. They conclude, rightly or wrongly, that their religious belief system caused their misery. Further, they discover that non-participation in formal religion *relieves* their symptoms. For example, since they give up belief or certitude of belief in an afterlife, they no longer worry whether they will burn in hell for some misdeed.

However, since in most cases these individuals also have some degree of OCD, they may continue to experience moral scruples as well as other symptoms. Thus, they may turn to religiously oriented counselors for help.

The methods for helping the agnostic are exactly the same as for helping the believer. The strategies of exposure and blocking work the same for both. The major difference is the *context* of the helping relationship. Pastoral ministers can be helpful to the agnostic if the person believes he or she will not be proselytized. Therefore, the major principle is that the religious counselor must respect the freedom of the person's belief system. Most religious counselors have little problem with this, since most adhere to the principle that belief is a free gift from God, and not something one can impose from the outside.

Once the person feels comfortable in the counseling relationship, the same change strategies for scruples will work. Occasionally, a person who works through the scruples may see that the problem was primarily psychological and that religion only provided the background for the scruples. In those instances, the person may seek further guidance for specific religious concerns. But, again, this needs to emerge from within the client and never be imposed or directed by the counselor.

## Scruples in the Unchurched

Sociologists of religion have their own precise definitions of who are the "unchurched." For our purposes the unchurched means people who remain believers yet are not participants in institutional religion. That is, they are not members of a church, synagogue, or similar institution. Or, if they are formally enrolled, they do not attend regular services.

I have observed clinically two categories of the unchurched in the area of scruples, although more surely exist. One group was raised in a denomination and still considers that faith group as home. The scruples, however, became so overwhelming that attending worship is a torment, so they ceased many, if not all, forms of external observance. Although they are not necessarily happy with this arrangement, they have come to accept it as their only reasonable alternative. A second group either was not raised in a particular faith group, or has discarded the belief as well as practices of religion in their family of origin. Although they no longer attend regular worship, they maintain an abiding faith in a personal God.

People with scruples from either group may seek help from religiously oriented counselors. The differences in helping manage the scruples are only slight and mainly follow the outline in Chapters 5–7. Essentially the unchurched may want to consider using attendance or participation in formal religious activities as a form of exposure. This may require reviewing the principles on developing motivation to change (Chapter 5). For persons in the first group, exposure is a stepping-stone to increased participation with their chosen faith group. Persons in the second group could view exposure primarily as a therapeutic activity and not as a prelude to formal enrollment in that faith group.

Obviously the person must decide what strategies to choose in overcoming scruples, and one's religious conscience will guide that choice in the unchurched as well as in regular attenders.

## Part Three

# PRACTICE AND THEORY OF CHANGING SCRUPLES

*Chapter 8*

## Getting Help for Scruples and OCD

The focus of this book is the specifically religious dimensions of obsessive-compulsive problems. For some persons these problems are developmental, are specifically religious, and will pass in time. For others, however, these problems continue, even though they may ebb and flow in intensity. In these cases the symptoms may be primarily or exclusively religious in content. More commonly, however, the scruples represent but one subset of obsessive-compulsive symptoms. As we have seen, many non-religious symptoms such as repeated washing, cleaning or checking for safety may also create considerable dysfunction for self and others. In these last two forms scruples represent one aspect of a larger health condition which is called OCD. We reviewed in Chapter 2 features of this condition. In this chapter we discuss resources for persons with scruples and OCD.

*Do I need professional help?* One should consider professional help in at least the following circumstances:

1. The symptoms have led to serious depression with thoughts about dying or urges to harm oneself physically.
2. The symptoms interfere with a sense of well-being or happiness.
3. The symptoms interfere with an occupation (paid employment, schoolwork, homemaker).
4. The symptoms interfere with interpersonal relationships (friendships, colleague, family living, intimacy issues).
5. The symptoms interfere with leisure time.

The last consideration is often noteworthy in OCD. Many can keep their lives together for a job or in external social situations, but take up most of their personal time with the symptoms.

*How do I find a helping professional?* The popularization of best-selling books (e.g. *The Boy Who Couldn't Stop Washing*), the openness of people with OCD appearing on popular television talk-shows (e.g. Oprah Winfrey), the establishment of a national self-help organization (Obsessive-Compulsive Disorder Foundation), and the promulgation of improved diagnostic and treatment methods to mental health professionals have all resulted in increased sensitivity and competence with treating the disorder.

A person with scruples and OCD probably has more competent help available than ever before. Although I still hear unfortunate stories of OCD clients with obvious symptoms misdiagnosed by therapists, fewer and fewer examples are of recent vintage. Nevertheless, a person with OCD needs to be an informed consumer.

An informed consumer of therapy services gathers as much information about the health care provider as is appropriately possible. One should feel free to question whether the therapist treats OCD regularly. In the case of scruples one should ask if the therapist is comfortable treating the religious aspects of the problem or willing to collaborate with a qualified religious consultant. Ask about the primary treatment method used in treating OCD by the therapist. Of course, one should know whether the therapist is a qualified, credentialed member of his or her profession. Credentialing bodies set up licensing, certification or membership criteria that set the standards for qualifications to provide services. We will review the different types of helping professionals in the next section.

If one chooses a therapist, it is appropriate to use the first few sessions to evaluate your ability to work with the professional. Potential problems in working together should be discussed openly to see how they can be resolved. An informed consumer is not the same, however, as hopping from therapist to therapist. Frequent changes in treatment providers may have more to do with a person's desire for quick relief than with the skills of the professional. Any reader who has attended to the behavioral change strategies discussed in this book realizes that change will not occur without perseverance and discomfort. Obviously no one can give an exact rule as to when "enough is enough" with a therapist, but exposure strategies and other treatments may take considerable time before relief occurs.

Finding a therapist depends on what the client needs. Despite differences in training among mental health disciplines, finding the right helper requires finding an experienced helper, not necessarily a member of a particular discipline (e.g. psychologist versus social worker). For example, three authorities in the OCD field are Judith Rapoport, Edna Foa, and Gail Steketee—a psychiatrist, psychologist, and clinical social worker, respectively.

A *psychiatrist* has a medical degree as well as extended training in mental health treatment. He or she is the only mental health professional who may independently prescribe medication. Some prospective clients prefer a psychiatric evaluation first to determine if medication might be helpful. Others prefer to try psychological methods first. We reviewed the research on the effectiveness of medication for treating OCD and scruples, which showed that many persons benefit from its use. Medication seems to help those in particular who have depression along with OCD. Some psychiatrists are qualified to employ the behavior therapy strategies we have described in this book. Others are not qualified, or have no interest in using behavior therapy, and limit their practices to supportive therapy, medication consultation and monitoring. These psychiatrists would refer their patients to other professionals for behavioral treatment.

*Clinical psychologists* hold a doctoral degree (in some states a master's degree plus extensive supervised experience) and are usually licensed in the state or jurisdiction where they practice. Some psychologists have a Ph.D., which means they have extensive training in research methods and have carried out independent research in addition to their extensive clinical training. Others hold a Psy.D. (Doctor of Psychology), which means they have extensive clinical training, but not the same requirements for carrying out independent research. Both Ph.D. and Psy.D. psychologists who practice independently require licensing or certification by the regional board which regulates the practice of psychology.

Psychologists are trained in the application of psychological principles in treatment. They are competent to do clinical assessments through the use of interview and psychological testing. They are also competent to diagnose and treat emotional problems. As in the case of psychiatrists, some receive training to administer the behavioral strategies for OCD. Others may be aware of behavioral methods, but are trained in a different model and do not employ them. The consumer must ask a particular psychologist if he or she uses behavioral methods to treat OCD, and not assume their use by virtue of the title of psychologist. A psychologist may not prescribe medication, and therefore,

together with the client, would need to determine the necessity of medication and make an appropriate referral to a psychiatrist. Psychiatrists
commonly collaborate with psychologists (or other professionals)
through medication consultation during simultaneous psychological
treatment.

*Clinical social workers* have a master's degree in social work
(M.S.W.), or a doctorate in social work (Ph.D. or D.S.W.). In addition,
they have specialized clinical training under supervision. They are
qualified to use psycho-social therapy methods and are also licensed or
certified in the jurisdiction in which they practice. As in the case of
other professions, a clinical social worker may or may not have
received training to use behavioral strategies to treat OCD. Again, one
needs to ask the clinical social worker if he or she has received specialized training or has appropriate experience.

*Certified or licensed counselors* have either a master's or a doctoral
degree in counseling, have extended supervised counseling experience
and have passed national or regional examinations for their profession.
A person may hold a counseling degree but not be certified because
either the region does not regulate counselors, or the counselor does not
have the necessary background. Counselors who do not have regional
certification often belong to a national organization which requires
passing a national examination (e.g. in the United States, the National
Board of Certified Counselors). Certified counselors are qualified to
use counseling strategies with their clients. Some counselors will have
specialized training in behavioral methods, some will have none. Some
counselors have extensive experience with major emotional difficulties
such as OCD. Others may have little or no experience. Again, the
potential consumer must ask.

*Psychiatric nurses* are registered nurses who have extensive supervised training and experience in psychiatric nursing. They also belong
to national and regional certification groups which have training criteria and require passing standardized examinations.

*Pastoral counselors* are not regulated by legal jurisdictions, but
belong to voluntary associations. The title pastoral counselor, then, may
be used in a variety of ways.[1] In the most loose sense, a pastoral counselor is someone who has completed theology training and counsels
people as part of his or her ministry. Pastoral counseling curriculum,
however, varies widely in theology training, with some programs offering many courses and others relatively few. Other programs (e.g. the

program the author is associated with) offer a master's or doctoral degree in pastoral counseling which is independent of ministry training for specific denominations. They include theology courses as well as extensive counseling training. Graduates have sufficient training to qualify as certified counselors (see description above). Pastoral counselors, with sufficient training and supervision, may join the American Association for Pastoral Counselors which sets standards and qualifies members according to expertise (Clinical Member, Fellow, or Diplomate). They conduct rigorous clinical examinations for membership. As with other disciplines the consumer needs to inquire whether the pastoral counselor has specialized training in the delivery of behavioral strategies for OCD treatment.

### Type of Treatment Available

*Medications.* In addition to counseling and support, psychiatric help may involve the use of medications to relieve scruples and other OCD symptoms. A full discussion of all medications which have been used to treat OCD is beyond the scope of this book. Nearly every medication available in the treatment of emotional problems has been tried at some time or another. We will limit this discussion to the common ones used today.

*Antidepressant* medications have an established track record for alleviating depression, and a number of specific compounds seem to benefit OCD. The antidepressant with the longest history in the treatment of OCD is clomipramine (Anafranil, USA). Although it resembles chemically a host of earlier antidepressants (e.g. imipramine), controlled research found that it helped OCD patients specifically. Researchers learned that clomipramine affects the central nervous system messenger chemical serotonin. More recently newer antidepressants which also work on the serotonin system have been used to treat OCD. Again, research has found two compounds effective: fluoxetine (Prozac) and sertraline (Zoloft).[2]

Antidepressants work slowly, usually taking two to three weeks before positive results are evident. One exception is sleep improvement which may occur more quickly. All medications have side-effects and the antidepressants are no exception. Lesser ones include dry mouth and possible drowsiness. Most side-effects disappear in time or else are easily tolerated. A few people may need to try several medications until they hit on one that works. We have a large number of available antidepressants, and effective medication is often found if the person is willing to cooperate with a trial-and-error approach. This approach is necessary because no method exists to determine in advance which medication will work for a given individual. Some investigators believe that antidepressant use in OCD is effective only if significant depression exists.[3]

No controlled study, to date, has examined whether one or another drug works specifically to eliminate scruples. One study, however, treated people with scruples with a variety of different antidepressant medications and found that the majority were helped significantly.[4] This study did not use a control group and looked at several medications, so we have less certainty about the effectiveness of any one compound. Nevertheless, this is a promising first step and justifies trying medication as one method to relieve scruples.

*Antianxiety* medications are often used to treat OCD because of the prominent role anxiety plays in the condition. These medications include the benzodiazapenes (Valium, Librium, Ativan, etc.), and a newer one which has similar properties—alprazolam (Xanax). Antianxiety medication relieves tension and reduces restlessness. The drawbacks include relapse of symptoms once the person stops the medication and potential addiction in a small percentage of cases. Since these medicines have withdrawal effects that range from mild to quite unpleasant, medical monitoring is required when the person stops using them.

*Behavior Therapy* is the other major treatment modality for OCD which controlled research has found effective. We have based most of the treatment strategies for scruples in this book on behavioral principles and have added specific suggestions from the history of pastoral care. Behavior therapy for OCD relies on the same concepts of exposure and blocking advocated throughout this book. Several publications of a self-help nature apply these strategies to OCD in general. The reader may find them quite valuable, and I have annotated some at the end of this chapter.

A behavior therapist's clinical training might include any of the professions described above. Psychologists are more likely to have this training than other professions, but many psychologists have not. The client must ask any therapist about specific training or expertise in behavior therapy. The Association for the Advancement of Behavior Therapy (see end of this chapter) provides referrals for North America from its membership list. Not every qualified behavior therapist belongs to this organization, but it is one place to start the search. Behavior therapy associations also exist in most countries that have professionally trained psychologists.

A *self-help* organization with thousands of members is the *Obsessive-Compulsive Foundation* (see end of chapter). They publish a newsletter (*The OCD Newsletter*), provide referrals for treatment professionals, and coordinate lists of local meetings for people with OCD. Many persons with scruples benefit from sharing their experiences with others. These meetings help reduce the stigma associated with the condition. A significant number of people with scruples have OCD and vice versa, so that support is usually available. The Foundation's newsletter announces innovations in the treatment of OCD as well as educational or media presentations about the disorder. It also contains first-hand accounts on how others cope with the problem.

*Scrupulous Anonymous* is an organization which publishes a newsletter of the same name (see end of chapter). The newsletter is published by the Redemptorist Fathers (founded by St. Alphonsus Liguori, an important figure in the Catholic moral theology tradition described in Chapter 4). The publication's pastoral bent is directed toward questions that seem mostly related to the Roman Catholic tradition, but is ecumenical in tone and content. It does not provide referral services. I have found the newsletter a useful adjunct to therapy for religious persons. Since the newsletter originates with religious authorities, it helps motivate clients to engage in the exposure and blocking strategies required for relief.

### Where To Find Help

*Professional Organizations.* Each professional group described above maintains a national office which provides names and addresses of members for a desired region. The following represent additional support services.

### Anxiety Disorders Association of America
6000 Executive Blvd. Rockville, MD 20852-3801
301-231-9350
Will provide lists of mental health professionals who have an interest and specialize in OCD.

**National Institute of Mental Health**
  9000 Rockville Pike. Building 10, Room 3D-41
  Bethesda, MD 20892 301-496-3421
  Coordinates ongoing research on OCD.

**OC Foundation**
  P.O. Box 70
  Milford, CT 06460-0070
  203-878-5669
  Self-help organization referred to at several points in the text. Provides names of mental health professionals interested in treating OCD. Publishes a newsletter about OCD. Provides information about the disorder to interested persons, and maintains lists of regional support groups.

**Obsessive-Compulsive Information Center**
  Department of Psychiatry, University of Wisconsin
  600 Highland Ave. Madison, WI 53792
  608-263-6171
  Publishes popular and technical information about OCD. Also will assist those seeking referrals.

**Scrupulous Anonymous**
  Scrupulous Anonymous/ Liguori, MO 63057
  Described above under self-help support. Publishes monthly newsletter.

  *Regional Professional Associations.* In some instances a regional professional association may be more helpful than a national one. Most state associations (e.g. Maryland Psychological Association) have referral services that are free to the public. In addition, treatment professionals often list their specialty with the local organization (e.g. anxiety disorders, or behavior therapy). Consumers can request providers by a specialty or interest. A consumer should check the white pages of the telephone directory for the state psychological, psychiatric, nursing association, etc.


### Recommended General Reading

See Reference Section for Complete Citation.

  Baer, Lee. *Getting Control: Overcoming Your Obsessions and Compulsions.* An excellent self-help book by a psychologist with extensive treatment and research experience. Includes detailed symptom checklists and easy-to-follow descriptions and explanations of exposure and blocking. He offers a number of valuable tips such as reminding us that we can control our behavior but not our urges and thoughts. Emphasizes the importance of working with a helper.

Rapoport, J. *The Boy Who Couldn't Stop Washing: The Experience and Treatment of Obsessive-Compulsive Disorder.* A best-selling work by a pioneer researcher in OCD at the National Institute of Mental Health (USA). Describes both medical and psychological interventions, but emphasizes the importance of considering medication for treatment of OCD. Has an impressive introduction to the discussion of scruples in the Appendix.

Steketee & White. *When Once Is Not Enough: Help for Obsessive Compulsives.* A superior self-help book which provides step-by-step instructions in the use of exposure and blocking to change obsessions and compulsions. It provides an updated description of OCD, and has a useful chapter on biological treatment as well. The first author participated in some of the better-conducted research projects which demonstrated the effectiveness of behavioral treatments for OCD.

Toates, F. *Obsessional Thoughts and Behaviour: Help for Obsessive-Compulsive Disorder.* An unusual and engrossing book by a British experimental psychologist who also suffers from OCD. The first half of the book is autobiographical and gives a vivid first-hand account of the impact of the disorder on this well-respected researcher and college professor. The second half of the book describes OCD in terms of what we know from biology and psychology. I particularly enjoyed the last few chapters which describe a number of literary figures who suffered from OCD, such as Hans Christian Andersen, John Bunyan, and Samuel Johnson.

### Readings from Technical Literature

Hundreds of technical articles appear annually and computerized searches greatly facilitate their discovery. Two searches often available to college or university libraries are *PsychLIT* from the American Psychological Association, and *Med-Line.* Below are a few books recommended as a start for understanding the technical literature in anxiety disorders or OCD specifically.

Rachman, S. J., & Hodgson, R. J. *Obsessions and Compulsions.* A comprehensive account of the clinical and scientific studies conducted in the treatment of OCD. The authors were pioneers in developing behavioral treatments for OCD and establishing their effectiveness when other approaches were having little or no impact. Generally considered a classic in the OCD field.

Marks, Isaac. *Fears, Phobias, and Rituals: Panic, Anxiety, and Their Disorders.* A colleague of Rachman and Hodgson, who has conducted OCD treatment research as well. He is an international authority in the field of anxiety and fear disorders. This book orients OCD in the larger picture of fear and anxiety disorders and contains several chapters devoted to OCD. A unique aspect to the text is its extensive consideration of the function of fear from an evolutionary perspective, and how fear and anxiety in humans resembles and differs from animals.

Barlow. *Anxiety and Its Disorders: The Nature and Treatment of Anxiety and Panic.* A comprehensive overview of the nature and treatment of anxiety and fear. Tends to give slightly more emphasis to theory than Marks, but reviews the clinical data in considerable detail. The OCD chapter is comprehensive and insightful.

*Chapter 9*

# Technical Asides: Moral Reasoning, Scruples, and the Psychology of Religion

### Scruples and Moral Reasoning

I have emphasized throughout this book the futility of attempting to convince someone to give up scruples through argumentation. Father O'Flaherty puts it sardonically: "The confessor has been infected [with vicarious scrupulosity] as soon as he starts to argue with the penitent about the innocence or guilt of a sinless sin."[1] Yet, using logical arguments or reasoning is often the first strategy tried by a religion professional in dealing with scruples. With this caveat in mind I still find it useful to orient the treatment of scruples within the broader domain of its role in moral reasoning.

Those who understand the core of scrupulosity as occurring at the emotional level will find this discussion unnecessary. Yet some have a keen interest in playing with ideas, and seem to benefit from an abstract description of moral reasoning and the fallacy of a scrupulous conscience. The helping person and those with scruples need to know that *this understanding alone rarely changes scrupulous behavior*, although it may motivate some to put forth greater effort in the psychological realm. I also find that this explanation is one that needs to be repeated periodically during treatment, and is best presented in bits and pieces as the person makes inquiries along the lines of ethical reasoning.

Some persons with scruples first see their problems as difficulties *with moral reasoning itself*. That is, they define the problem as cognitive and religious. They see themselves as unable to make moral decisions with enough certitude to act freely in some instances. They either heard or have a conviction that "no one should act with a doubtful conscience."[2] Believing strongly in this principle they find themselves frequently unable to resolve doubts. This dilemma paralyzes them or consumes them with guilt if they feel forced to act.

To escape the dilemma some visit religious counselors, read books on ethics or moral theology, or attempt to develop a highly refined set of rules about moral behavior. As a result of this search, they raise interesting questions about moral reasoning, some of which have tantalized thinkers for centuries.

Such discussions with clients, along with consulting ethical philosophers, helped to clarify the ultimate futility of resolving scruples through moral reasoning. This chapter discusses the nature of moral reasoning (within a theistic framework) and the role of scrupulosity in that reasoning process. The conclusion I reach is that attempting to solve ethical issues from a scrupulous foundation creates an infinite loop of further difficulties for the person.

## The Nature of Moral Reasoning

I rely heavily on Albert Jonsen and Stephen Toulmin's engrossing history of moral reasoning.[3] Their framework allows us to pinpoint the core problem with scrupulosity. What follows in this section highlights issues relevant to understanding scruples.

According to Jonsen and Toulmin, western moral thought provides at least two major views of moral reasoning. One view wants moral reasoning to achieve the degree of scientific certitude that is similar to mathematics. In this view moral reasoning proceeds like Euclidian geometry: universal absolute principles (axioms) lead to logical and certain theorems. The morality of an individual act should logically lead back to some universal principle, thereby determining its appropriateness. Problems in deciding the morality of an act are related to deciding which universal moral principle is involved. The classical proponent of this view was the philosopher Plato, and it was developed further by Descartes. Descartes, curiously enough, was trying to provide a rigorous scientific basis for moral behavior against the skeptics of his day. So he used a basically geometric model to help establish moral rules as deriving from "self-evident" truths.

A different view was taken by Plato's contemporary, the Greek philosopher Aristotle. In this view, moral reasoning is scientific in a different sense. The first position sees ethics as scientific in the *theoretical* sense, in the same way as mathematics. That is, once terms are defined, conclusions follow inevitably from the rules of logic. Aristotle proposed that ethics is scientific in a *practical* sense. For example, ethics is more similar to the practical sciences such as medicine. In a practical science, one applies a variety of different principles or strategies to *individual cases.*

In practical sciences appeal to universal truths is of little use if the investigator has misdiagnosed the case. What matters most is a careful delineation of all the *circumstances* surrounding the case. After careful examination of the case, the next decision is which principle to apply. The case may be very similar to other cases (paradigms) or unique. For paradigmatic cases readily available principles or treatments usually exist. For unique cases the best one can do is apply analogous principles from the most similar circumstances. The authors conclude that *ethics can never be a demonstrative science*, but must proceed from a different methodology.

What, then, is the methodology of ethics? A group of moral philosophers developed a methodology known as *casuistry*, which emphasized ethics as a practical science, one that needs to take into account the concrete circumstances in determining the moral nature of behavior. Of course, some casuists went too far, as the authors admit, and generated arguments along the line of how-many-angels-can-dance-on-the-head-of-a-pin? This led to religious reformers and philosophers repudiating the entire system. The methodology itself is not at fault, precisely because ethics is not a deductive science. As ethicists today are discovering in trying to resolve complex ethical problems (e.g. organ transplantation, prolonged life-support systems, etc.), nothing is gained by throwing the baby out with the bathwater. Indeed, casuists use several methods to resolve moral questions, and by following Aristotle's model come to practical moral conclusions.

We will see that when people use these strategies to solve moral problems (and we naturally do, even if we do not allude to the philosophical considerations behind them), they create core conflicts with scrupulosity. Casuistry employs six basic strategies.

1) *Paradigm and Analogy.* Although universal principles are difficult to find in ethics, paradigm cases can be found. These are cases on which nearly universal agreement exists as to their moral nature (e.g. killing the innocent). Moral reasoning uses these paradigms (modern thinkers might call them prototypes) and then argues from them by way of *analogy* to a current case.

Abortion represents one such perplexing problem that some have tried to resolve using paradigm and analogy. Everyone agrees that killing the innocent is wrong. Some see abortion as identical to the paradigm of killing the innocent. Others see it only as analogous. For example, fetal life may not be "innocent" if the mother's life is in danger. To others, if the fetus is not viable outside the uterus, it is "life" only analogously with limited rights. Or, abortion is not a paradigmatic case because it becomes a clash of "rights," i.e. between the mother and the fetus. The controversy continues because proponents of one side or the other cannot find a mutually agreeable paradigm on which to base consensual laws or practices.

2) *The Use of Maxims.* Over the centuries a variety of maxims were used as short-cuts in ethical reasoning. Some may have been biblically-based (e.g. the ten commandments). Others represent a more common-sense approach (e.g. force may be repelled by force). We use maxims in our daily transmission of ethical values, both in the home and in formal settings. My six year old son likes to quote one regularly, "If you can't say something nice about someone, don't say nuttin."

3) *Circumstances.* Classical authors (Aristotle, Cicero) and medieval casuists agreed that "circumstances make the case." All may agree that killing the innocent is wrong. But is a burglar in my house innocent and deserving to die under the following scenarios? First, a masked burglar is armed with a knife, has it raised, and is standing over my eight year old daughter's bed. Or, second, the burglar looks to be about ten years old and is walking out of my house with my video game collection.

We may not like having to dissect the circumstances of ethical choices in this manner, but reason dictates that universal rules are not much help in these instances. It is easy to poke fun at the excesses of casuistry, but all engage in weighing circumstances when evaluating human acts.

4) *Probability.* By now the reader unfamiliar with the history of moral reasoning may have concluded exactly what professional moral philosophers know. Given the need to argue from analogy rather than paradigms in most instances, the usefulness of maxims, and the critical nature of circumstances, complete certitude in determining the morality of an act is often impossible. Does that mean we are all in the same dilemma as the scrupulous? Always needing to act with a doubtful conscience?

Ethical theory went beyond this dilemma by introducing the notion of probability. If only a few human acts are intrinsically evil and paradigmatic, many ethical conclusions will have only a degree of certitude. To prevent moral paralysis the theologians argued that we are free to act even if we do not have exact certitude. All that is required is that we have a "probable" degree of certitude. "Probable" had its own technical meaning. It does not have our modern connotation of plausible. Rather, it meant that a person used accepted methods in weighing the human act, and these methods allowed one to conclude that the act was permitted. But—*and here is the crucial point for scrupulosity*—one could act with this probable certitude.

Some philosophers and theologians eventually rejected "probabilism," as it came to be called, because they felt it degenerated into hairsplitting. But, as Jonsen and Toulmin point out, the options then are only a rigorous "safe" position or a lax one. This is precisely the dilemma of the scrupulous: they will not choose a lax position, but cannot find a safe one. Most ethicists use probability in moral judgment whether acknowledged or not, unless they are complete situationists or rigorists.

5) *Cumulative Arguments.* If ethics is a practical science, seldom does one argument provide the "knockout punch" in resolving a dilemma. Rather, arguments evolve from many different viewpoints and methods. In medicine a diagnosis in fuzzy cases results from analyzing many pieces of information, with no one item being conclusive. In this book I used that method to distinguish developmental scrupulosity from clinical scrupulosity. At a given point in time developmental scrupulosity might be identical to the clinical version. But when all the diagnostic criteria are considered, they justify a separate category. The same holds for ethical decisions. Leave out one argument and the act looks wrong; add one more and weight shifts to acceptance.

6) *Resolution.* Casuists believed that one could not act with a doubtful conscience, so they made a point in resolving ethical dilemmas. As we have repeated, ethics is a practical science and should provide advice on how to act. The casuists would provide such advice usually by noting whether an action was probable and to what degree. Probable meant that sufficient evidence existed for a person to act with a clear conscience. It did *not* mean that a person had total absolute certitude such as exists in mathematics. But this is acceptable because practical sciences related to human actions will never have this degree of certitude.

## Applications to Scrupulosity

The point of reviewing this method of moral reasoning is not to convince readers to adopt casuistry. Rather, it highlights the complexity of moral reasoning and the inherent ambiguity in decision-making. Using this framework we can appreciate the multiple avenues of uncertainty for the scrupulous during the moral reasoning process.

*Paradigm versus analogy* creates dilemmas for the scrupulous in distinguishing the nature of a moral act. Is *any* sexual feeling or response the same thing as impurity? Unable to make that determination, some opt for the safest position. As a result they live in terror of the continual bombardment by modern media through sexual salesmanship. They walk down the street with eyes downcast to avoid gazing upon an attractive person. Others watch television with the remote control in hand to switch channels instantly when spotting an alluring image. They cannot distinguish prototypical impurity, dishonesty, maliciousness, etc., from the wide range of messy but tolerable human experience. As the medieval casuists knew, the price of total safety in moral behavior is the confinement and loss of freedom which comes with scrupulosity.

*Maxims become laws.* Maxims, as noted above, are quite helpful in the guidance of everyday moral behavior. They have a folksy, down-to-earth quality that makes them particularly useful for education and storing in memory. How often in the course of a week do we automatically play one or more in our heads? For example, "One good turn deserves another." A person with scruples, however, tends to treat maxims as *absolute universal laws*, and lock in on a maxim to the exclusion of other considerations.

Biblical language is a case in point. Scripture scholars for centuries commented on the importance of understanding the literary style of biblical authors to interpret a passage correctly. The use of hyperbole is a simple example: "If your right hand causes you to sin, cut it off and throw it away" (Matthew 5:30). Even Christian groups which promote literal biblical interpretation know that obedience to these maxims would leave their followers blind and maimed.[4] The scrupulous are unable to discern the *guiding, educative* role of maxims and biblical sayings. Once again, in their drive for absolute certainty, the maxims become universal laws admitting no exception.

*Circumstances* often create painful dilemmas for the scrupulous. They have great difficulty in appreciating how circumstances can change the very nature of an act—for example, the moral duty that we love our neighbor as ourselves. When do we do this, where, under what circumstances, or, as was asked of Jesus, "Who is our neighbor?"

> John worked in a huge government agency that employed thousands. He believed that loving one's neighbor meant he was obligated to greet with a "Good morning" or nod of his head each and every worker he passed. He could pass, conceivably, hundreds of persons any time he stepped out of his office. If he missed greeting someone, he felt an impulse (and sometimes acted on it) to circle the corridor to catch up with and greet the person. Using the biblical story of the good Samaritan in which Jesus answered the question of who is one's neighbor, he eventually realized that, when walking the corridors, he only had to extend himself to those in true need. This "solution," however, generated a whole new set of problems in dealing with the dozens of homeless and panhandlers who accosted him on his daily ride on the subway. Were not these people modern-day equivalents of the victim in the good Samaritan story? Did he have to contribute money to each? Later, he was helped to resolve this issue, when one afternoon he spotted one of the regular "cripples" at his subway stop walking rapidly down the street with his crutches slung over his shoulders.

*Probability* rather than absolute certitude represents the greatest dilemma in scrupulosity. As Judith Rapoport points out, OCD is a "doubting disease." Sufferers lose their ability to know that they know.[5] Since moral certitude is not the same as theoretical, mathematical certitude, our moral "knowing" has a degree of ambiguity. Each human act represents the choice of one good out of many possible ones. A scrupulous person requires complete conviction that the act is *the best possible* so that he or she feels free of the torment of doubt.[6]

A brilliant literary description of this dilemma is reflected in the obsessive-compulsive meandering of Sylvia Plath's narrator in her famous novel *The Bell Jar*.[7] The narrator is an intelligent, gifted writer, yet living in post-World War II, in an era with limited opportunities for creative women. As she considers her career options she describes her confusion using the branches of a fig tree for her metaphor. Exploring the fruit of one branch, i.e. choosing one career option, means cutting herself off from tasting the other fruits. She contemplates being a wife and mother, a poet, a professor, an editor, an Olympic champion, a traveler to exotic places, a lover of offbeat men. These options triggered paralysis not challenge.

> I saw myself sitting in the crotch of this fig tree, starving to death, just because I couldn't make up my mind which of the figs I would choose. I wanted each and every one of them, but choosing one meant losing all the rest, and, as I sat there, unable to decide, the figs began to wrinkle, and go black, and, one by one, they plopped to the ground at my feet (p. 85).

Many moral decisions are similar. Is my choice to use time and energy to write this book the best moral one I could make? Are other projects more worthwhile? Given that scrupulosity represents a problem for perhaps one percent of the population, should I not work on a project with wider application? Should I be spending more time with my family? Sleep later in the morning for health or stress reduction reasons?

With the exception of characters in existential novels and drama, few people agonize over these decisions unless the situation is momentous. Whether we choose to agonize over the decisions or not, however, the inherent moral ambiguity exists. Most of us accept emotionally the "probable" certitude of our acts and move on. We may regret for a moment (or longer) that we cannot explore every branch, but in the end we act.

Some of the behavioral strategies we have proposed for helping scruples are geared toward just this point. We recommend activities which are ambiguous on purpose, so that the person learns to tolerate the "probability" of moral certitude rather than its absolute nature. Once an activity is "permitted," the person attempts it, even if it represents less than the ideal.

Finally, scruples frequently prevent *resolution* of the moral dilemma. Requiring absolute certitude prevents a person from enacting a permitted behavior. A person may refuse a promotion because of imagined ethical conflicts associated with the position. Close friendships may be avoided for fear of "sinning." A person may stop praying for fear of "bad thoughts."

## Scruples, Religion, and Causality

Having examined the phenomenology of scruples from a theological, ethical, and psychological perspective, we may perhaps be excused the temptation to address once again the question of whether religious belief causes scruples. I wish to provide only the bare outline of a response, and a more complete one awaits empirical research in the domains of the psychology and sociology of religion.

In my opinion we can reliably identify at least three types of scrupulous behavior.[8] *Developmental scrupulosity* (Type I) is known in both spiritual theology and developmental psychology.[9] Spiritual theology indicates that this is common at two developmental stages. The first stage is during adolescence. For a significant minority scrupulosity may appear as an over-sensitivity to newly emerging identity issues, and represents conflict between freedom and personal responsibility. As we have indicated, scruples in these phases generally pass with guidance and support from health mentors or with the passage of time. The change strategies for scruples suggested in this book should be helpful for this type, although we have no controlled research to confirm this. Adolescents who have persistent scruples that are not amenable to standard guidance require referral to qualified mental health specialists.

The second developmental point identified as a possible trigger for scruples occurs following a religious conversion in adulthood. This may happen if the new religious awareness represents a dramatic behavioral contrast to a former way of life. For example, those who saw themselves as great sinners before their conversion may over-react emotionally to sin as a result of their new spiritual awareness. This was the case with St. Ignatius Loyola following his conversion, as we noted earlier.[10]

*Milieu-influenced* scruples (Type II) represent another version. As religious history and clinical observations confirm, scruples can be taught. The major systems that can teach scruples are family and religious educators. Scrupulosity pared down to its basic emotional ingredients represents a fear response. Empirical research demonstrates that fear responses may be learned in multiple ways from the environment.[11] We learn to be afraid through direct experience *and* through others. Emotionally significant authority figures who transmit a strong fear component in their message will trigger emotional arousal in their students. This arousal may then generalize, through the laws of learning, to the broader category of moral decision-making itself. Scrupulosity, then, may develop when the person learns that bad thoughts will be punished or that only perfection pleases God.[12]

Milieu-influenced scruples differ from those associated with OCD in that the concern or fear is a shared one within the person's reference group. The fear orientation in morality represents either a majority or a significant minority within the believing group. For these persons moral behavior is not a joyous seeking out of the good, but a preoccupation with avoiding evil. They would not have what St. Paul has described as "the freedom of the glory of the children of God."

A disturbing example of milieu-influenced fear that, to my knowledge, is not specifically labeled as scruples involves sexual fears. The medical team of William Masters and Virginia Johnson report the one variable most associated with treatment failure of sexually dysfunctional couples was religious orthodoxy.[13] Conservative Catholic, fundamentalist Protestant, and Orthodox Jewish couples represented the bulk of their treatment failures. Theorists who speculate on the emotional processes of fear reduction believe that intense fear reactions to the fearful situation may predict treatment failure.[14] We may speculate that the intense sexual fear for the couples who failed to benefit from Masters and Johnson's exposure therapy was mediated by religious instruction.[15]

Another example of milieu-influenced scruples mentioned in classical theology is extreme physical deprivation. This probably accounts for few cases today, but it highlights the importance of considering biological influences. Spiritual writers cautioned about the hazards of extreme rigor (severe fasting or bodily mortifications). Rigor, in their opinion, "dried up the brain" and interfered with judgment. Ironically, a great deal of research now goes on to measure brain chemicals that may be associated with OCD.[16]

Milieu-influenced scrupulosity, since it relies on modeling selective behavior, has great variability. One religious group may be rigorous in one dimension of ethical practice, but tolerant in another. An adolescent in one group may fret that applying make-up is a sin, and not worry about masturbation, while a youngster in another group has the opposite pattern. People who remain in these organizations may never develop scruples in the sense described in this book.

Milieu-influenced scruples cannot just fall along dimensions of liberal-conservative practices within a religious group.[17] As with other scruples, the predominant characteristic driving the practice is a fear orientation, a worry component that pervades and overshadows other areas of moral behavior.

People with this form of scruples have three possible outcomes. Some accept this orientation as normative for their faith system and adapt as best they can. Others experience it as burdensome and leave the organization. Still others remain in their faith group but change their belief or approach to the moral issues to one devoid of fear.

*Clinical scrupulosity* (Type III) represents that version associated with the symptoms of OCD, and which we described in detail in Chapter 3. Religion simply represents one part of the cultural context for the expression of the symptoms.

Psychiatrist David Greenberg supplies several criteria to identify clinical scruples from standard religious practices.[18] 1) The religious drive in scruples is narrow. That is, it focuses on one area of morality to the exclusion of equally or more central beliefs. The person might be obsessed with having impure thoughts but show little or no interest in works of charity. 2) The moral concern may play a trivial role for the faith group. A man obsesses over a drop of holy water hitting the floor when entering the church. 3) Scruples may interfere with normative religious practice. A woman stops going to synagogue for fear of having blasphemous thoughts there. 4) Often scrupulous rituals are resisted, whereas religious rituals are usually desired. Most believers have some interest in the religious practices of their group. A person with scruples has no intrinsic interest in repeating prayers by the hour to atone for or neutralize an obsession. A contemplative nun, on the other hand, might set aside several hours daily for prayer to pursue her goal of union with God. 5) Finally, in clinical scrupulosity one almost always sees other OCD symptoms.

In clinical scrupulosity religion simply represents the cultural backdrop for the symptom expression. An American paranoid schizophrenic may believe the CIA is following him; in another country it might be the secret police. Spy agencies do not cause paranoia as a disease, although fear tactics may cause a cultural paranoia. To follow this analogy, milieu-influenced scrupulosity is to clinical scrupulosity what cultural paranoia is to paranoid schizophrenia.

This analysis illustrates the multifaceted relationship between religious practice and scruples. In type I, religion plays an important role in the sense of providing a contrast with a former or newly emerging way of life. In type II, religion plays a role through instruction and rule-governing advice from the reference group. In type III, religion designs the shape of the pathological symptoms rather than causing their origin.

Conceptual support for this position may be gleaned from two sources. Greenberg and Witztum point out that rituals are common in several major world religions.[19] This raises two possibilities, in their opinion: 1) ritualized religion predisposes people to OCD, or, 2) ritualized religion predisposes people to develop OCD versus another disorder. My suggestion is that each is true. What I call milieu-influenced scrupulosity involves a fear-driven mode of transmitting religious instruction which predisposes members to scrupulosity, even though the reference group may not view the behavior as excessively rigorist. Clinical scrupulosity, on the other hand, would result from ritualized religion predisposing to OCD versus another disorder. Or, as noted above, ritualized religion provides the backdrop but is not the cause of OCD.

Support for my proposed categories arises also from emotion theory which suggests that specific anxiety disorders are not transmitted genetically in families, but that a generalized tendency for anxious over-arousal is inherited. Cultural and environmental factors (such as religion) would then influence the particular manifestation of the disorder.[20]

This theory, then, would predict that heredity plays a larger role in the development of clinical scrupulosity, and social learning predominates in milieu-influenced scrupulosity, although both factors might exist to some degree for each type. One savvy moral theologian reasoned similarly in a practical way. If a religious counselor interviews one hundred students in a religious college, for example, the counselor could expect one or two students to have scrupulosity. If the number is closer to seven, then he advises looking around for some environmental source.[21]

## What Religion Can Learn
## from the Psychology of Scruples

The desire to integrate psychology and theology (and spirituality) has caused an explosion in theoretical and applied work.[22] This book has attempted to expand the repertoire of each discipline by applying change strategies from one content area (behavioral psychology) to problems associated with a different domain (religious practice and symptomatology).

Until now the psychological models that religious practitioners have relied on are mainly psychoanalytic, Jungian, or existential-humanistic ones. Pastoral ministry has benefited from the applied insights of each. However, they do not represent the only models from modern psychology which have utility for the integration of psychology and religion. Nor do they even represent the dominant models in academic psychology.

The reasons for this lack of interest are manifold. Academic psychology relies heavily on experimental methods, in which few pastoral ministers or theologians have training. Second, behaviorism, with its specter of Watson and Skinner, represents a deterministic position that is not amenable to religious viewpoints.[23] Third, psychologists as a group are not members of formal religious groups to the same degree as persons in the general population.[24] Finally, the negative bias toward behaviorism by theology has perhaps kept the field uninformed about the "cognitive revolution" in behavioral approaches which leaves ample room for freedom.[25] If this book's approach seems cogent to those in the religious disciplines, perhaps it will generate greater openness to the benefits of the proposed psychological model.

Specifically, then, religious studies may benefit from the study of scruples in several ways. The effectiveness of behavioral methods for treating scruples and OCD demonstrates that psychological models are, when all is said and done, only models. Unlike theological models, they need not have any intrinsic ties to orthodox positions. They arise out of the scientific method and either are useful for understanding and predicting human behavior or they are not. If they are not, in time they will be discarded (or, at a minimum, ignored).

Just as behavioral science need not be tied down to one particular model, the practical discipline of pastoral ministry need not adopt one model from the behavioral sciences. When professional therapists are polled regarding their theoretical orientation, the majority describe themselves as eclectic. That is, they do not belong to one "school" of opinion, but use a variety of strategies from several models. Eclectic integration, however, requires careful thought. One is reminded of Arnold Lazarus' statement that an eclectic is a person who has both feet planted firmly in the air!

The field of pastoral ministry and pastoral counseling, although it may strive for integration of psychology and religion at the theoretical level, derives no benefit from adopting any single model for pastoral practice. This holds particularly for those aspects of pastoral practice which utilize techniques from the discipline of counseling.[26]

The study of scruples, then, with emphasis on behavior therapy strategies, should drive this notion home. In behavior therapy we have a model for understanding *and* changing scruples. Previous models simply have not worked. In a fine example of openness to psychology, *The Treatment of Scruples*, a book over thirty years old, applied the then-current model (psychoanalysis) to understanding scruples. A lengthy article by a psychiatrist explained the clinical understanding of scruples using a psychoanalytic framework. A doctrinal history review by theologian A. Tesson examined seventeenth and eighteenth century moral theology positions on scruples.

Tesson is completely mindful of the psychiatric nature of the disorder and the understanding brought by clinical methods. Nevertheless, when he compares the standard centuries-old pastoral guidelines for scruples (e.g. complete obedience to a spiritual guide) to the then-available treatment (psychoanalysis), he concluded his review with a perceptive and pessimistic comment: "In this respect, can we claim that we have made any very great progress."[27] This comment precedes behavior therapy with OCD and illustrated the ineffectiveness of available treatment.

Does this mean that behavior therapy should become the dominant model for pastoral ministry? Not necessarily. But it illustrates the potential usefulness of a neglected body of work by those in religion. And, since pastoral ministry is a practical discipline, I find it difficult to believe that our current knowledge-base would support *any* dominant model. But the effectiveness of behavior therapy for certain kinds of psychological problems (e.g. anxiety and fear disorders) provides an ethical challenge to pastoral ministry. Given their proven effectiveness, can educators for pastoral ministry ethically withhold this information in training, or remain uninformed about the strategies themselves? Further, is it conscionable to teach clinical-pastoral methods which exclude these strategies?

## What Psychology Can Learn from the Study of Religious Scruples

At the same time, the field of abnormal psychology has something to learn from the study of scruples. As Foa and her colleagues observe, not all OCD symptoms are equally responsive to standard behavior therapy.[28] They point out that OCD characterized by *overvalued ideas* represents a resistant form of the disorder. Overvalued ideas refer to obsessions which do not always seem senseless to the person. Clinical practice views overvalued ideas as somewhere on the border between obsessional thinking (which sees the idea as senseless or irrational) and delusions (a totally false perception, e.g. believing your mail-carrier is a CIA agent).

My opinion, based on the clinical and theoretical aspects of scruples, is that scruples are resistant to change *because their religious nature places many of them in the domain of overvalued ideas.*[29] In other words, the person sees that the stakes are so high in religious doubt (i.e. salvation depends on being correct), that the senselessness of the behavior is less evident. After all, faith itself implies looking beyond sensory experiences and the surface meaning of reality. Scrupulous people usually know that their peers do not act the way they do. But since religious salvation is such an individual experience, can one really take a chance and ignore that "inner voice"? Therefore, the religious aspects of scruples create a motivational drive around the symptoms which become overvalued ideas, and hence resistant to change.

The field of abnormal psychology, therefore, could learn from the wisdom of pastoral practice in handling these overvalued ideas. In an earlier chapter we noted psychiatrist Greenberg's technique for implementing exposure and blocking in religious persons—that is, consulting with a spiritual authority first to find out if a particular strategy is permitted. This incorporates both the wisdom of past pastoral practices (obedience to a spiritual authority) and behavior therapy (exposure and blocking). This may suggest an important approach to the treatment of overvalued ideas, a combination of authority and behavioral practice. Empirical studies could be devised to test this approach.

Clinical work also requires validation of counseling methods that make explicit use of clients' religious perspective. This research is long overdue, and some preliminary work indicates the utility of this approach. Rebecca Propst and her colleagues studied treating depressed patients who had a religious orientation. They found that incorporating the clients' religious beliefs through either cognitive-behavior counseling strategies or standard pastoral counseling methods led to more rapid recovery than standard counseling methods *without* using the clients' religious beliefs. What is even more intriguing is that using the clients' religious beliefs was effective even if the counselors *were agnostic themselves!*[30]

The scientific study of scruples, therefore, will enrich both abnormal psychology and pastoral counseling. I hope this book has demonstrated that current therapeutic methods allow us to move beyond Father Tesson's gloomy conclusion thirty years ago that we are hardly better off in managing scruples than we were in the seventeenth century. All behavioral research, to date, has focused on religious obsessions and compulsions only in the context of OCD, so we still need to validate the methods specifically for scruples. However, since clinical scrupulosity simply provides the context for the broader problem of OCD, we have little reason to doubt their effectiveness. The fact that medications which are specific to OCD alleviate scruples confirms this optimism.[31]

At the same time much remains unknown. Our pronouncements about the biological origins of the disorder still remain highly speculative despite the incredible sophistication of biochemistry and brain-imaging technology. Nevertheless, the development of bio-psycho-social-spiritual approaches in the past ten to fifteen years holds much promise for understanding this troubling disorder. This book will have succeeded if it encourages persons with scruples and those entrusted with their care to examine carefully available change strategies.

# A Step-by-Step Treatment for Scrupulosity

### Step One: Identifying Scruples

I. The definition of scruples includes both obsessions and compulsions.
   A. Obsessions: repeated thoughts, images, urges or acts which *trigger* anxiety.
   B. Compulsions: repeated acts, thoughts or images which *reduce* anxiety.
   C. Scruples are obsessions and compulsions with religious content.
      1. Or, seeing sin where there is none.

II. Since obsessions and compulsions are normal for most people, what criteria are used to define them as a problem?
   A. Frequency: How often? Once a week versus ten times daily.
   B. Intensity: Annoying versus creating severe anxiety.
   C. Duration: A fleeting thought versus lasting for long periods.
   D. Interference: How much do they interrupt daily living or preferred activities?
   E. Resistance: Easy to dismiss versus unable to get rid of them.

### Step Two: Self-Monitoring

I. Keep a daily record of obsessions and compulsions.
   A. Figure A-1: Daily Record of Obsessions and Compulsions.
   B. What to record?
      1. Circumstances surrounding the scrupulous events.
         a. External circumstances: Who, what, when, where, why, and how.

    b. Internal circumstances: Your state of mind, mood, feeling, what you were saying to yourself.

  2. Intensity of the anxiety.

    a. Scale of 1–10.

      (1) See scale description at bottom of Record Sheet.

  3. Amount of time the obsession and compulsion lasted.

  4. Examples on Figure A-2.

### Step Three: Developing Motivation to Change

I. List all the reasons for changing your scruples.

  A. Figure A-3: Personal Motivation List.

    1. Write in top box the *benefits* of change.

      a. E.g. anxiety relief, time for positive activities, a sense of personal freedom, how your loved ones or friends will view you, reducing your sense of embarrassment.

      b. Emphasize the positive *feelings* you are likely to experience from changing your scruples.

    2. Write in the lower box the *costs of not changing*.

      a. Living in continual fear and anxiety; time taken from family, job, hobbies, duties, etc.; impaired religious devotion; constant fear of God's punishment; loss of freedom.

      b. Emphasize the negative *feelings* associated with not changing the scruples.

    3. Examples on Figure A-4.

### Step Four: Targeting Obsessions for Change

I. From the Daily Record Sheet list the major obsession on the Target Obsessions List (Figure A-5).

  A. Rate the degree of anxiety that each obsession generates *on the average*.

    1. Examples on Figure A-6.

  B. From the Target Obsessions List select the obsession that generates the least amount of anxiety, on the average.

  C. Transfer that obsession to the first line of the Worksheet for Changing Obsessions (Figure A-7).

  D. Now break down the obsession into a range of situations.

    1. See examples on Figure A-8.

E. Break down each obsession on a separate Worksheet for Changing Obsessions.

    1. Each situation you list should *provoke* some anxiety, even if only a little.

    2. Generate up to ten situations that provoke anxiety for that situation, ranging from mild to intense.

F. This will provide you with a large number of situations for exposure therapy.

### Step Five: Obtaining Permission To Enact Exposure Strategy

I. If you are concerned that placing yourself in situations that trigger your obsession may not be morally permissible, then an in-between step is required.

    A. You must give yourself permission to expose yourself to the situation triggering the scruple.

        1. For example, you may tell yourself, "I know doing this *feels* wrong, but I *know* this is morally permissible."

II. Or, you will need to find a religious expert of your choosing whose advice you are comfortable following.

    A. Take your Worksheet for Changing Obsessions (and the Worksheet for Changing Compulsions noted below), and ask the expert to review each situation.

        1. The question for the expert is to evaluate each situation and answer the question, "Is it permitted for me to do . . . ?"

        2. If the expert deletes a situation, ask his or her help in suggesting an alternative—one that will also provoke anxiety for you.

### Step Six: Targeting Compulsions for Change

I. From the Daily Record Sheet list the major compulsions on the Target Compulsions List (Figure A-9).

    A. Rate the degree of anxiety that each compulsion generates *on the average*.

        1. See the bottom of the List for a scale description.

            a. Examples of this are on Figure A-10.

    B. From the Target Compulsions List select the compulsion that generates the least amount of anxiety on the average.

1. Transfer that compulsion to the first line of the Worksheet for Changing Compulsions (Figure A-11).
   a. Break down that compulsion into a range of situations, and rank each situation according to the degree of anxiety generated.
      (1) Example in Figure A-12.
C. Repeat that process for each compulsion on the Target Compulsions List.
   1. Each situation you list should *provoke* some anxiety, even if only a little.
   2. Generate up to ten situations that provoke anxiety, ranging from mild to severe.
D. This will provide you with a large number of situations for blocking strategies.

## Step Seven: Obtaining Permission To Enact Blocking Strategy

I. As described in Step Five, either give yourself moral permission actually to carry out the blocking strategy for each situation, or else consult a religious expert of your choosing.
A. Follow the process outlined in Step Six.

## Step Eight: Putting it All Together—Obsessions *Plus* Compulsions

I. Identify *external* compulsions or rituals for change first.
A. Determine what is "normal" regarding the amount and frequency of the targeted behavior.
   1. Find a "prudent guide" and stick to that advice.
      a. For example, washing hands before meals (no longer than one minute), or after using the bathroom (again, one minute).
      b. Use that advice as your goal or criterion.
II. Select an obsession with compulsion from the Worksheet for Changing Compulsions.
A. Start with an obsession and situation that generate a low level of anxiety.
B. *Expose* yourself to the situation triggering the obsession for blocks of time up to 90 minutes.
   1. *Without performing the ritual or compulsion.*

  2. Repeat this process until the anxiety is in the none to mild range, and the urge to perform the compulsion is under control.

 C. Then, move on to the next most anxiety-provoking obsessional situation and repeat the exposure plus blocking the ritual.

III. For "stand alone" obsessions, i.e. those that do not have compulsions or rituals attached.

 A. *Expose* yourself to the least anxiety-provoking obsession from the Target Obsessions List.

  1. Stay in the situation for a period up to 90 minutes, until the anxiety falls into the mild or none range.

  2. When repeated exposures generate manageable anxiety, move on to the next most anxiety-provoking obsession and repeat the process.

 B. Aids to the exposure process include:

  1. A kitchen timer or a wrist watch that has a beeper alarm.

   a. For example, set the timer for a five minute prayer session, then stop when it goes off.

  2. "Remote Control" strategies by which you arrange your environment to prevent a ritual from happening.

   a. For example, have someone present to distract or encourage you.

   b. During the day, lock the bathroom door that has the shower, and leave the key with a companion or friend.

   c. Tell people what you are going to do, and ask if they will listen to your progress, and perhaps read your Worksheets.

## Step Nine: The Reporter Strategy for Unacceptable Experiences

I. For feelings, ideas or images that are "forbidden" or unacceptable.

 A. For example, jealousy, anger, sexual arousal.

  1. When suppression just seems to increase the frequency or intensity.

  2. But suppression does not work, and makes the ideas more forceful.

II. "Reporter" strategy tends to defuse and interrupt the feeling.

 A. And, at the same time avoids "giving in" or acting out the unacceptable impulse.

  1. (In reality, the feelings are neutral and normal, but trying to

change these feelings through rational persuasion seldom works.)

III. When you become aware of the emotion, idea or impulse that "feels" wrong, imagine that you are a newspaper reporter.

  A. Imagine your assignment is to write a brief paragraph in your mind (or on paper, if that helps).

    1. Describing the experience in a detached, objective manner.

    2. Ask the questions—who, what, when, where, why, how, how often, how much, etc.—about the experience.

    3. Keep describing it mentally (or in writing).

    4. Practice on something neutral.

      a. Example, *lacing and tying shoes.*

      (1) ("I see two brown shoes on the floor, and I reach first for the left one. I slowly loosen the laces, and notice that the ends of each lace are slightly frayed. The brown of the lace is somewhat darker than the tone of the shoe itself. The heel is considerably worn and the front and back have notable scuff marks that are a much lighter color than the non-scuffed sections. The shoe slips comfortably over my foot, and then I feel a sharp, tiny pain at the toe. I remove the shoe and shake out a small pebble caught from a walk in the park yesterday. The shoe goes back on, this time with no obstruction. I take the lace in my right hand and lace first one side, then the next, up to the top eyelet. I pull tightly on the laces, one end in each hand, until I feel considerable pressure on my instep, etc.")

  B. Describe the *experience, not the conflict.*

    1. Example of a sexual conflict when seeing an attractive person: ("There is an attractive person, wearing brown shoes, and carrying an umbrella. There is some sexual interest on my part (about a 5 on a scale of 1-10). He/she is walking down the street in an obvious hurry toward the bus stop. The bus stop sign is about six feet high, is round, and has the words printed in green capital letters. He/she turns to greet a waiting passenger. Both smile, and begin a conversation, etc. I'm noticing that my sexual interest has decreased slightly as the bus arrives and picks up the passengers.")

      a. Other example in Chapter 7.

  C. Avoid focusing on the *conflict* itself.

    1. For example, avoid internal dialogue like the following:

        a. "Oh, no, I'm feeling attracted and wonder if I'm going to get aroused, and if that happens am I going to be able to control my thoughts. Why did I have to even see such a good-looking person today? Everything had been going well."

  D. Example of an *anger* scenario.

    1. "The baby's crying woke me up again. I need to change her diaper, and I'm exhausted. I'm noticing that I am quite angry (7 on a scale of 1-10). I'm trying to keep my eyes open in the dark so I don't awaken anyone else with turning on the light. I reach the baby's room and turn on the light. She has buried her head in the corner of the crib and is wailing furiously. She actually looks kind of pathetic, like a beached whale. I pick her up and her crying slows down. I put her on the changing table and notice that she is now looking at me and smiling. I am very sleepy and imagine how pleasant it will be to go back to bed. I take off the diaper, etc. I notice my anger has decreased somewhat (to a 3)."

  E. Keep describing the event/scenario until you are more in control of your worries about the feelings that are emerging.

    1. Stop when acceptance outweighs the fear or anxiety.

IV. Reporter strategy is *not* a substitute for exposure or blocking.

  A. It is to be used for those spur-of-the-moment surges of fear that you are losing control.

    1. It needs to be supplemented by working on the target obsessions and compulsions noted above.

  B. Exposure and blocking get at eliminating the main themes and categories of your scruples.

    1. Reporter strategy can help you feel comfortable when overwhelmed by an immediate feeling.

**Figure A-1**
**Daily Record of Obsessions and Compulsions**

| Date | Situation | OBSESSION:<br>Thought, image, impulse or behavior that *triggers* anxiety | Tension Level 1 - 10 | COMPULSION:<br>Thought, image, impulse or behavior that *reduces* anxiety | Time spent dealing with obsession and/or compulsion |
|---|---|---|---|---|---|
|  |  |  |  |  |  |

From:  Joseph W. Ciarrocchi, Ph.D.
*The Doubting Disease*
Paulist Press

Copy worksheet for personal or therapeutic use.

**Figure A-2**
**Daily Record of Obsessions and Compulsions**

| Date | Situation | OBSESSION: Thought, image, impulse or behavior that *triggers* anxiety | Tension Level 1 - 10 | COMPULSION: Thought, image, impulse or behavior that *reduces* anxiety | Time spent dealing with obsession and/or compulsion |
|------|-----------|-----------------------------------------------------------------------|----------------------|-----------------------------------------------------------------------|-----------------------------------------------------|
|      |           |                                                                       |                      |                                                                       |                                                     |
|      |           |                                                                       |                      |                                                                       |                                                     |

From: Joseph W. Ciarrocchi, Ph.D.
*The Doubting Disease*
Paulist Press

Copy worksheet for personal
or therapeutic use.

**Figure A-3**
**Changing Scruples**
**Personal Motivation List**

| Benefits of eliminating scruples | 1. |
| | 2. |
| | 3. |
| | 4. |
| | 5. |
| | 6. |
| | 7. |
| | 8. |
| | 9. |
| | 10. |
| Costs of not changing scruples | 1. |
| | 2. |
| | 3. |
| | 4. |
| | 5. |
| | 6. |
| | 7. |
| | 8. |
| | 9. |
| | 10. |

## Figure A-4
## Changing Scruples
## Personal Motivation List

| Benefits of eliminating scruples | 1. More time for family and fun. |
| --- | --- |
| | 2. Kids will enjoy me more. |
| | 3. I will feel less anxious. |
| | 4. I can attend worship again. |
| | 5. I will be at peace with God. |
| | 6. |
| | 7. |
| | 8. |
| | 9. |
| | 10. |
| Costs of not changing scruples | 1. Strange looks from loved ones. |
| | 2. I embarrass my family. |
| | 3. Very restricted activities. |
| | 4. Waste a lot of time. |
| | 5. Always making excuses to others. |
| | 6. People avoid me. |
| | 7. |
| | 8. |
| | 9. |
| | 10. |

## Figure A-5
## Target Obsessions List

**OBSESSION:** Thought, image, impulse or behavior that *triggers* anxiety.

Average Tension
Level

1. _____

2. _____

3. _____

4. _____

5. _____

6. _____

7. _____

8. _____

9. _____

10. _____

**Tension Level**

| | | |
|---|---|---|
| 1 | = | No anxiety |
| 2-3 | = | Mild anxiety |
| 4-5 | = | Moderate anxiety |
| 6-7 | = | Severe anxiety |
| 8-10 | = | Intense anxiety |

**Guidelines:**
Work first on obsession that generates *least* amount of tension, on average. (Do not obsess if some are very close. Pick any one, flip a coin, etc.)

From: Joseph W. Ciarrocchi, Ph.D.
     *The Doubting Disease*
     Paulist Press

Copy worksheet for personal or therapeutic use.

**Figure A-6**
**Target Obsessions List**

---

**OBSESSION:** Thought, image, impulse or behavior that *triggers* anxiety.

| | Average Tension Level |
|---|---|
| 1. Angry with spouse; God will punish me | 7 |
| 2. Store clerk returned too much change | 8 |
| 3. "Love of neighbor" means greeting everyone | 5 |
| 4. Idea to hit people when I cross a busy street | 7 |
| 5. Urge/idea to make obscene phone call | 9 |
| 6. Idea of running people down with my car | 8 |
| 7. Thought that God is really the Evil One | 10 |
| 8. Playing with my child may physically injure her | 6 |
| 9. | |
| 10. | |

**Tension Level**
1    = No anxiety
2-3  = Mild anxiety
4-5  = Moderate anxiety
6-7  = Severe anxiety
8-10 = Intense anxiety

**Guidelines:**
Work first on obsession that generates *least* amount of tension, on average. (Do not obsess if some are very close. Pick any one, flip a coin, etc.)

From: Joseph W. Ciarrocchi, Ph.D.
        *The Doubting Disease*
        Paulist Press

Copy worksheet for personal or therapeutic use.

**Figure A-7**
**Worksheet for Changing Obsessions**

**Day/Date**

| Obsession: | Exposure Strategy: | Guidelines: |
|---|---|---|
| Disturbing thought, doubt, activity, or impulse that *triggers* anxiety. | 1) Spend 15-90 minutes staying in situation that triggers obsession.<br><br>OR<br><br>2) Intentionally provoke the obsession and dwell on it for 15-90 minutes. | 1) Stay in situation or think about obsession until tension level drops to mild range.<br><br>Scale<br><br>1 = No anxiety<br>2-3 = Mild anxiety<br>4-5 = Moderate anxiety<br>6-7 = Severe anxiety<br>8-10 = Intense anxiety<br><br>2) If anxiety becomes intense, consider "reporter" strategy while dwelling on obsession. |
| | Initial Tension Level 1-10 | Amount of time spent exposed to obsession | Final Tension Level 1-10 | |

Copy worksheet for personal or therapeutic use.

From:   Joseph W. Ciarrocchi, Ph.D.
        *The Doubting Disease*
        Paulist Press

**Figure A-8**
**Worksheet for Changing Obsessions**

**Day/Date**

| Obsession: | Exposure Strategy: | | | Guidelines: |
|---|---|---|---|---|
| Disturbing thought, doubt, activity, or impulse that *triggers* anxiety. | 1) Spend 15-90 minutes staying in situation that triggers obsession. OR 2) Intentionally provoke the obsession and dwell on it for 15-90 minutes. | | | 1) Stay in situation or think about obsession until tension level drops to mild range. |
| | Initial Tension Level 1-10 (7) | Amount of time spent exposed to obsession | Final Tension Level 1-10 (3) | Scale<br>1 = No anxiety<br>2-3 = Mild anxiety<br>4-5 = Moderate anxiety<br>6-7 = Severe anxiety<br>8-10 = Intense anxiety |
| Spouse forgot my birthday. I got angry, then worried he would die in an accident as God's punishment to me. | For 30 minutes I thought about him being killed or injured. | | | 2) If anxiety becomes intense, consider "reporter" strategy while dwelling on obsession.<br><br>I tried to focus on the physical details of the scenes. |

From:  Joseph W. Ciarrocchi, Ph.D.
       *The Doubting Disease*
       Paulist Press

Copy worksheet for personal
or therapeutic use.

**Figure A-9**
**Target Compulsions List**

**COMPULSIONS:** Thought, image, impulse or behavior that
*reduces* anxiety.

                                                    Average Tension
                                                        Level

1. _____
2. _____
3. _____
4. _____
5. _____
6. _____
7. _____
8. _____
9. _____
10. _____

**Tension Level**
1     = No anxiety
2-3   = Mild anxiety
4-5   = Moderate anxiety
6-7   = Severe anxiety
8-10 = Intense anxiety

**Guidelines:**
Work first on compulsion
that triggers *least* amount
of tension, on average. (Do
not obsess if some are very
close.)

From: Joseph W. Ciarrocchi, Ph.D.
        *The Doubting Disease*
        Paulist Press

Copy worksheet for
personal or therapeutic use.

**Figure A-10**
**Target Compulsions List**

---

**COMPULSIONS:** Thought, image, impulse or behavior that *reduces* anxiety.

|  | Average Tension Level |
|---|---|
| 1. Praying for spouse so that he or she doesn't die | 7 |
| 2. Checking grocery receipts for mistakes | 8 |
| 3. Greeting everyone "hello" as sign of charity | 5 |
| 4. Hold package in hands to prevent hitting anyone | 7 |
| 5. Cover telephone to prevent obscene phone call | 9 |
| 6. Drive slowly to not hit people | 8 |
| 7. Long prayers at thought, "God is Evil" | 10 |
| 8. Check child's condition repeatedly when playing | 6 |
| 9. | |
| 10. | |

**Tension Level**
1   = No anxiety
2-3  = Mild anxiety
4-5  = Moderate anxiety
6-7  = Severe anxiety
8-10 = Intense anxiety

**Guidelines:**
Work first on compulsion that triggers *least* amount of tension, on average. (Do not obsess if some are very close.)

From: Joseph W. Ciarrocchi, Ph.D.
      *The Doubting Disease*
      Paulist Press

Copy worksheet for personal or therapeutic use.

**Figure A-11**
**Worksheet for Changing Compulsions**

| Day/Date | Exposure Strategy: | Compulsion: | Guidelines: |
|---|---|---|---|
| | Think about or place yourself in situations that trigger disturbing thought, impulse, image or ritual. | Thought, image, impulse, or act that *reduces anxiety.* | 1) Stay in situation until tension level drops to mild range. |
| | Describe situation or thought. | *Blocking Strategy: Do the Opposite.*<br>1) If impulse to *avoid* object or activity—*DO IT.*<br>2) If impulse to do something: e.g. repeat, check, pray, seek reassurance—*prevent the response.* | Scale<br>1 = No anxiety<br>2-3 = Mild anxiety<br>4-5 = Moderate anxiety<br>6-7 = Severe anxiety<br>8-10 = Intense anxiety |
| | | Initial Tension Level 1-10 / Amount of time spent exposed to situation / Final Tension Level 1-10 | 2) If anxiety becomes intense, consider "reporter" strategy while staying in situation. |

From:  Joseph W. Ciarrocchi, Ph.D.
 *The Doubting Disease*
 Paulist Press

Copy worksheet for personal or therapeutic use.

**Figure A-12**
**Worksheet for Changing Compulsions**

**Day/Date**

| Exposure Strategy: | Compulsion: | Guidelines: |
|---|---|---|
| Think about or place yourself in situations that trigger disturbing thought, impulse, image or ritual. | Thought, image, impulse, or act that *reduces* anxiety.<br><br>*Blocking Strategy: Do the Opposite.*<br>1) If impulse to *avoid* object or activity—*DO IT.*<br>2) If impulse to do something—e.g. repeat, check, pray, seek reassurance—*prevent the response.* | 1) Stay in situation until tension level drops to mild range.<br><br>Scale<br>1 = No anxiety<br>2-3 = Mild anxiety<br>4-5 = Moderate anxiety<br>6-7 = Severe anxiety<br>8-10 = Intense anxiety |
| Describe situation or thought. | Initial Tension Level 1-10 (6)    Amount of time spent exposed to situation    Final Tension Level 1-10 (3) | 2) If anxiety becomes intense, consider "reporter" strategy while staying in situation. |
| Playing "piggyback" or "rough-house" with my two-year old child. | Played for 20 minutes with her, and did not ask her if she was all right. | I tried to listen to her giggling and laughter as a distraction to my anxiety. |

From: Joseph W. Ciarrocchi, Ph.D.- *The Doubting Disease* - Paulist Press — Copy worksheet for personal or therapeutic use.

# Obsessions and Compulsions Checklist

Patient Name_____  Date _____

| **AGGRESSIVE OBSESSIONS** | **Current** | **Past** |
|---|---|---|
| • Fear might harm others | | |
| • Fear might harm self | | |
| • Violent or horrific images | | |
| • Fear of blurting out obscenities or insults. | | |
| • Fear of doing something embarrassing | | |
| • Fear will act on other impulses (e.g. to rob bank, to shoplift, to cheat cashier) | | |
| • Fear to be responsible for things going wrong (e.g. company will go bankrupt because of patient) | | |
| • Fear something terrible might happen (e.g. fire, burglary, death or illness of relative/friend, miscellaneous superstitions) | | |
| • Other | | |

| **CONTAMINATION OBSESSIONS** | | |
|---|---|---|
| • Concerns or disgust with bodily waste or secretions (e.g. urine, feces, saliva) | | |
| • Concern with dirt or germs | | |
| • Excessive concern with environmental contaminants (e.g. asbestos, radiation, toxic wastes) | | |
| • Excessive concern with household items (e.g. cleansers, solvents, pets) | | |
| • Concerned will get ill | | |

|  | Current | Past |
|---|---|---|
| • Concerned will get others ill (Aggressive) | _____ | _____ |
| • Other | _____ | _____ |

## SEXUAL OBSESSIONS

|  | Current | Past |
|---|---|---|
| • Forbidden or perverse sexual thoughts, images, or impulses | _____ | _____ |
| • Content involves children | _____ | _____ |
| • Content involves animals | _____ | _____ |
| • Content involves incest | _____ | _____ |
| • Content involves homosexuality | _____ | _____ |
| • Sexual behavior toward others (Aggressive) | _____ | _____ |
| • Other | _____ | _____ |

## HOARDING/COLLECTING OBSESSIONS  _____  _____

## RELIGIOUS OBSESSIONS  _____  _____

## OBSESSIONS WITH NEED FOR SYMMETRY, EXACTNESS OR ORDER  _____  _____

## MISCELLANEOUS OBSESSIONS

|  | Current | Past |
|---|---|---|
| • Need to know or remember | _____ | _____ |
| • Fear of saying certain things | _____ | _____ |
| • Fear of not saying things just right | _____ | _____ |
| • Intrusive (neutral) images | _____ | _____ |
| • Intrusive nonsense sounds, words, or music | _____ | _____ |
| • Lucky/unlucky numbers | _____ | _____ |
| • Colors with special significance | _____ | _____ |
| • Other | _____ | _____ |

## SOMATIC OBSESSIONS/COMPULSIONS  _____  _____

## CLEANING/WASHING COMPULSION

|  | Current | Past |
|---|---|---|
| • Excessive or ritualized handwashing | _____ | _____ |
| • Excessive or ritualized showering, bathing, toothbrushing, or grooming | _____ | _____ |
| • Involves cleaning of household items or other inanimate objects | _____ | _____ |
| • Other measures to remove contact with contaminants | _____ | _____ |

|                                                              | **Current** | **Past** |
|--------------------------------------------------------------|-------------|----------|
| • Other measures to remove contaminants                      | _____     | ____     |

### COUNTING COMPULSIONS

|                                                              | **Current** | **Past** |
|--------------------------------------------------------------|-------------|----------|
| • Checking doors, locks, stove, appliances, emergency brake on car, etc. | _____ | ____ |
| • Checking that did not/will not harm others                 | _____     | ____     |
| • Checking that did not/will not harm self                   | _____     | ____     |
| • Checking that nothing terrible will happen                 | _____     | ____     |
| • Checking for contaminants                                  | _____     | ____     |
| • Other                                                      | _____     | ____     |

### REPEATING RITUALS

|                                                              | **Current** | **Past** |
|--------------------------------------------------------------|-------------|----------|
| • Going in/out door, up/down from chair, etc.                | _____     | ____     |
| • Other                                                      | _____     | ____     |

### HOARDING/COLLECTING COMPULSIONS

| | **Current** | **Past** |
|-|-------------|----------|
| | _____     | ____     |

### ORDERING/ARRANGING COMPULSIONS

| | **Current** | **Past** |
|-|-------------|----------|
| | _____     | ____     |

### MISCELLANEOUS COMPULSIONS

|                                                              | **Current** | **Past** |
|--------------------------------------------------------------|-------------|----------|
| • Mental rituals (other than checking/counting)              | _____     | ____     |
| • Need to tell, ask, or confess                              | _____     | ____     |
| • Need to touch                                              | _____     | ____     |
| • Measures to prevent: (not checking)                        |             |          |
|   harm to self                                     | _____     | ____     |
|   harm to others                                   | _____     | ____     |
|   terrible consequences                            | _____     | ____     |
| • Other                                                      | _____     | ____     |

From: Yale-Brown Obsessive-
       Compulsive Scale. Used with
       permission.

# Notes

## 1. Scrupulosity: An Overview

1. Carroll, 1964.

2. *American Heritage Dictionary*, 1991, p.1104.

3. Simpson (1960), p.540. *Scrupus* is a sharp stone; *scrupulus* is its diminutive; *scrupulosus* is the adjective meaning exact, accurate, precise, or full of sharp stones.

4. Peele (1989) effectively critiques society's propensity to use disease models to explain away social problems or escape from personal responsibility. He weakens his complaint considerably with his off-handed and sarcastic remarks that the government has just "discovered" a new disease affecting millions—namely obsessive-compulsive disorder. In reality, the condition has been known for centuries (see Chapters 2 and 3), and the disorder is crippling to many of its victims. Most sufferers would rightly resent their condition being compared to the outrageous extension of the disease model such as the "Twinkies" defense which claimed that the murderer of a San Francisco council member was "insane" at the time from eating too much junk food. Because mental illness may have its shades of gray does not exclude the existence of black and white.

5. Casey, 1948.

6. Marks, 1978; Miller, 1979; Miller & Munoz, 1976.

7. Bergin holds that this may be partly attributed to the demographic

differences between mental health professionals and the general public. He cites evidence that an overwhelming number of Americans believe in a personal God (91%), but significantly fewer therapists do (79%). For some professions the rates are even lower, e.g. psychologists (70%) compared to social workers (90%). [Bergin, 1991]

8. Religious believers who follow the tradition of behavior therapy usually distinguish *radical* behaviorism from *methodological* behaviorism (Craighead, Kazdin & Mahoney, 1976). Radical behaviorism accepts the philosophical roots of John Watson and B. F. Skinner (e.g. Skinner, 1972), maintaining that all behavior is environmentally determined, and that human freedom is an illusion, although a necessary one. Methodological behaviorism maintains belief in personal freedom but accepts behavioral methods as a useful technology for understanding the principles of human behavior and change. The irony of using the deterministic heritage of Pavlov, Watson, and Skinner to develop effective strategies for a religious/emotional problem follows the medieval tradition of using truth from any source (e.g. Aristotle) to illuminate our faith experience. Deterministic roots should not deter religious counselors, because pastoral counseling began by attempting to integrate Freudian thinking (which is also deterministic) within a pastoral care perspective (Estadt, Blanchette, & Compton, 1991).

### 2. Scruples and Obsessive-Compulsive Disorder

1. One commentator on the *Spiritual Exercises* of St. Ignatius Loyola observes: "Properly speaking, the temporary lack of certitude and firmness of judgment aroused by this experience is not scrupulosity. Instead, this is recognized traditionally as a symptom of growth.... We desire to move beyond the now-recognized dullness or obtuseness of our conscience because we are roused by a new sensitivity of love" (Fleming, 1978, p.229).

2. Bainton, 1950.

3. Fleming, 1978.

4. Barlow, 1988; Foa *et al.*, 1983; Marks, 1987; Rachman & Hodgson, 1980; Steketee & White, 1990.

5. Karno, *et al.*, 1988; Myers, *et al.*, 1984; Regier, Narrow, & Rae, 1990.

6. American Psychiatric Association, 1987 (definition of obsession); Marks, 1987 (definition of compulsion).

7. Rachman and Hodgson identified these five types from their factor analytic studies of OCD patients. Researchers have proposed other typologies. Akhtar *et al.* (1975) divide obsessions into obsessive doubts, obsessive thinking, obsessive fears, obsessive impulses, and obsessive images.

8. Myers *et al.*, 1984; Marks, 1987. A less likely explanation is that women with severe OCD do not seek help as readily as men. This contradicts the consistent data which sees women, across all diagnostic categories, as greater "help-seekers" than men. It would mean that for this one condition women behave differently. A more technical explanation suggests sampling bias (less likely for ECA survey, but more reasonable for treatment studies). Many factors account for why a particular clinic or agency is selected by patients, and thus data from individual treatment centers may not represent gender ratios in the population at large.

9. Greenberg, Witztum & Pisante, 1987.

10. A Japanese study of children found that girls had an earlier onset contrary to North American and European studies (Honjo, Sugiyama, Ohtaka, Aoyama, Takei, Inoko & Wakabayashi, 1989). We do not know, therefore, how culture influences the decision to obtain help for children with OCD symptoms.

11. First degree relatives include biological parent, child or full sibling. For reviews see Last & Strauss, 1989; Minichiello *et al.*, 1990; and Rasmussen & Tsuang, 1986. One study found 36 percent of first degree relatives of OCD patients had a diagnosable mental condition compared to 17 percent of a matched group of non-clinic people (McKeon & Murray, 1987).

12. Whitaker *et al.*, 1990.

13. Karno *et al.*, 1988.

14. Cited in Barlow, 1988, p.1.

15. Turner, Beidel, & Stanley, 1992.

16. Rapoport, 1990.

17. The human mind is amazingly fertile, so that clinicians encounter obsessions that often defy categorization. One person would freeze before tossing a paper towel in a lavatory wastebasket, not because of germ phobia, but because of some unspecified sexual connotation. Another was drawn to pornography because of the obsession that he did not "understand" female anatomy.

18. Rasmussen & Eisen, 1990.

19. OCD differs from hypochondriasis (excessive concern about health) in that OCD usually focuses on a single symptom or disease. For example, a person may obsess about cancer alone (OCD), whereas a hypochondriac is afraid across all systems.

20. This last case easily fits in with psychoanalytic concepts such as "reaction formation," which suggest that the mother's overconcern about hurting the child represents a defense against her unconscious wish not to have the child. These interpretations, like many psychoanalytic concepts, are extremely difficult to prove one way or another. My only response is to point to the immense relief she feels after undergoing exposure treatment.

21. Rasmussen & Eisen, 1990. As in the case of obsessions, researchers have different typologies.

22. Rachman & de Silva (1978). The authors sampled a non-random group of 124 persons. Another study suggests it takes longer to dismiss intrusive thoughts bcause they are harder to ignore than neutral thoughts (Edwards & Dickerson, 1987).

23. Freud held that anxiety or a phobia is only an outward manifestation of a hidden anxiety that accounts for the worry. In the case of

OCD, Freud viewed anxiety as self-directed aggression to punish oneself for prohibited desires during the sadistic anal stage (around ages 2-3). Even practicing psychoanalysts admit the limited benefit of psychoanalysis in treating long-standing OCD (Lauras, 1964).

24. Barlow, 1988. See the annotation on this book in Chapter 8.

25. Psychoanalytic thinkers refer to this as *magical thinking*. That is, the person believes that thoughts or mental experiences have a true external reality.

26. Wegner, 1989.

27. Some speculate that cognitive deficits are at the heart of OCD. Do people with OCD check repeatedly because of faulty memories for whether a task was completed? A series of studies with non-clinical checkers and non-clinical washers drew the following conclusions: 1) checkers are slower to categorize objects into groups than washers; 2) checkers are not different in long term memory recall (e.g. naming past presidents of their country); 3) checkers have better attention spans; 4) checkers have poorer memory for prior action, and difficulty distinguishing whether a behavior actually occurred or was just a thought; 5) checkers perform more poorly on tasks requiring recall of details of meaningfully linked sequences (e.g. a short paragraph in story form); and 6) checking is associated with a broad range of psychological syndromes in a non-clinical population. A study with a clinical sample found that checkers had memory deficits for recently completed actions (Frost *et al.*, 1988; Frost & Sher, 1989; Frost, Sher & Green, 1986; Sher *et al.*, 1983, 1989, 1991; Sher, Mann & Frost, 1984). The authors suggest that checking might represent attempts to regain a sense of control over one's environment. My own hypothesis is that perhaps cleaning is related to *fear*, i.e. a present danger, but checking is related to *anxiety*, i.e. a vague threat.

28. In diagnostic terminology the obsessions in OCD are *ego-alien* or *ego-dystonic*. Desiring a sports car is *ego-syntonic*.

29. This analysis is based on Borkovec *et al.* (1983), Craske *et al.* (1989), and Turner, Beidel & Stanley (1992).

30. The official psychiatric diagnostic manual (DSM III-R, American Psychiatric Association, 1987) labels these under Axis Two, to distinguish them from disorders that have less to do with one's personal behavioral *style* and are more characterized by specific symptoms (e.g. alcoholism, depression, eating disorders, etc.). These disorders are coded under Axis One. Rates of specific personality disorders in OCD vary from study to study. Although some studies found high rates of obsessive-compulsive personality disorder in OCD patients, the majority have not. For a review of the relationship between OCD and obsessive-compulsive personality disorder see Steketee, 1990.

31. For technical reviews see Mavissakalian, Hamann, & Jones, 1990a, 1990b; Pfohl *et al.*, 1989; Pollak, 1987; Stanley *et al.*, 1990; Steketee, 1990.

32. Marks (1987); Martinot *et al.* (1990); Rapoport (1990).

33. Neale & Liebert, 1986.

34. Baer, 1992

35. Biographers note that St. Ignatius Loyola used a close variant of exposure and blocking to handle his own scruples, a method one author refers to as "a blitz procedure" (O'Flaherty, 1966, p.4).

36. Foa *et al.*, 1983.

37. Christiansen *et al.*, 1987; Marks *et al.*, 1988; Steketee & Tynes, 1991.


### 3. Scruples: Common and Uncommon

1. I am grateful to a member of the national Obsessive-Compulsive Disorder Foundation (cf. Chapter 8), who several years ago called my attention to Bunyan and even sent me his book as a gift after reading an article on scrupulosity I had written for their newsletter. All quotes are from Bunyan, 1988.

2. The reader who is further interested in historical examples might wish to pursue the writings and biographies of Bunyan's British secular

counterpart, Samuel Johnson, who apparently suffered from OCD. Johnson, for example, was known to have a complicated ritual for passing through doorways (Boswell, 1968).

3. Bainton, 1950.

4. Answering these questions has a long history in Christian theology in the branch known as *Apologetics*.

5. "Therefore, I say to you, every sin and blasphemy will be forgiven people, but blasphemy against the Spirit will not be forgiven" (New American Bible, 1988). I have encountered numerous examples of this obsession clinically and in casual contact with religious persons. One father had an eighteen year old son with this obsession, and the father alone had contacted numerous pastors and religious counselors for information about the sin. Both father and son believed that the problem was simply one of actually discovering what the sin was, and if they could do that, then the son would be reassured he was blameless. When I crossed paths with them, they were in search of a biblical scholar who could read and interpret the meaning of Jesus' words in the original Aramaic and thus give them guidance. I suggested unending theological pursuit would be fruitless for relieving the doubt.

6. Or, ego-dystonic in the technical language of psychopathology.

7. This worry about "consenting" to wicked thoughts is one that plagues persons with scruples, as we will see in the next section.

8. No longer being able to cry represents a deeper form of clinical depression; cf. the Beck Depression Inventory (Beck *et al.*, 1961).

9. Even though historically we have had self-help organizations for nearly every problem imaginable, only most recently have sufferers gone public. See Chapter 8, for example, regarding the Obsessive-Compulsive Disorder Foundation. This tendency to isolate has a profound negative effect, and reduces the chances that people will seek help.

10. Barlow, 1988.

11. Meissner, 1992, p.76.

12. Vita of St. Ignatius, as quoted in Meissner, 1992, p.76. Meissner, writing in the psychoanalytic tradition, describes this as a "transference cure" (p.80). Learning theory, as we will propose throughout this book, offers an alternative explanation.

13. *Autobiography*, as quoted in Caraman, 1990, p. 39.

14. O'Flaherty, 1973.

15. For religious persons a "collaborative" coping style may actually have the most positive benefit for overall mental well-being. Recent work, for example, suggests that believers who are under high stress and see themselves as working with God toward solutions have fewer depressive symptoms than those who believe it all depends on themselves or it all depends on God (Bickel, 1993).

### 4. Scruples in the History of Pastoral Care

1. The theologians, of course, were well aware of the ambiguity of moral events. To handle this ambiguity, yet allow for human action, the theologians distinguished various degrees of certitude. Rules and principles were offered on how one could develop moral certainty about particular acts. This is discussed in more detail in Chapter 9.

2. Jone & Adelman, 1959.

3. In preparing this book I visited a seminary library for research materials and met some seminarians who were close to ordination. When they inquired about my research I told them it was about scruples. They all admitted not knowing the meaning of the word. This may reflect the pastoral decline in handling the problem since the practice of confession has radically diminished since the end of the Vatican Council. What was once a monthly practice for many Catholics may be annually or less. Speculation on the decline is often linked to Pope Paul VI's letter condemning birth control (Paul VI, 1968). Scruples in the Catholic Church, then, may be in decline due to changed religious practices. Research on this issue could highlight the relationship between environmental settings and the development of psychological symptoms.

4. Some behavior therapy strategies originate in social learning theory which refers to this form of learning as modeling, e.g. Bandura, 1986.

5. As noted in Rapoport, 1990. Rapoport maintains that Freud's view on this matter is not an attack on religion. However, this view plus his well-known position on belief in God as an "illusion" put many religious thinkers on guard against the fields of psychiatry and psychology.

6. Arterburn & Felton, 1991; Booth, 1992.

7. Greenberg, 1984; Greenberg & Witztum 1991.

8. Fleming, 1978.

9. I find the continuation of the pastoral tradition intriguing especially because it ran counter to the prevailing clinical *Zeitgeist*, i.e. psychoanlysis. A French study of scruples co-authored by a psychoanalyst and theologians thirty years ago examined the intricate relation between the religious content of scruples and obsessive-compulsive disorder (Carroll, 1964). The theologian, Fr. Tesson (1964), in a remarkably perceptive essay, points out that the major pastoral practice for treating scruples (blind obedience to a religious director) has no ready explanation for its effectiveness in psychoanalytic terms. Behavioral theory today, in contrast, would see the church's practice as creating the motivation for the person to practice exposure which is the core of fear reduction. Fr. Tesson also laments that the clinical and pastoral practices of his day have not advanced much beyond fifteenth century pastoral guidelines. We take this issue up in Chapter 9.

10. Jesuit moral theologian O'Flaherty (1966, 1973) outlines a number of strategies for treating scruples which follow the church's pastoral tradition, yet in a systematic way that resembles behavior therapy. He does not explicitly reference behavioral treatments (which would have been meager for OCD at the time he wrote), but his common sense approach anticipates some components. Curiously, his work receives favorable citation from clinical specialists in OCD (e.g. Rapoport, 1990; Greenberg, 1984), but is little referenced in Catholic pastoral training. This may reflect, as noted earlier, the decrease in frequency of confession and changes in moral theological emphasis since the late 1960s.

### 5. Targeting Scruples and Developing Motivation

1. Rachman, 1976; Foa & Kozak, 1991.

2. Wegner, 1989.

3. Wegner, 1989, p.182.

4. Prochaska & Di Clemente, 1986. I am indebted to William Miller's lucid application of this model and the centrality he gives to motivational interviewing (Miller & Rollnick, 1991). Another psychologist who has given this topic much thought, but approaches it from a slightly different angle, is Donald Meichenbaum. His popular workshops on cognitive-behavior modification provide many clinical examples of employing "reactance" theory (Brehm, 1966) in the clinical setting. Reactance is the psychological set we use to resist being influenced by others. Reactance allows us to survive daily life in which we are bombarded literally by hundreds of messages (thousands for TV viewers!) to comply with others' wishes. This set also works against us when we *should* change. Psychoanalysis has called this set *resistance* and it has special meaning in their formulations. Meichenbaum, Miller and others in the tradition of cognitive-behavior therapy see resistance as the manifestation of reactance as studied in social psychology. Meichenbaum and Turk (1987) applied motivational strategies from a slightly different literature designed to enlist maximum patient cooperation in their book *Facilitating Treatment Adherence*.

5. An excellent analysis of Alcoholics Anonymous' spiritual dimension is Ernest Kurtz' *Not God* (1979). AA uses the paradox of surrender as its central core. Surrender may work particularly well specifically because it de-emphasizes the notion of will power. As suggested by Wegner (1989), the more we try to exercise mental control intentionally the less successful we are with obsessional ideas.

6. E.g. Miller & Rollnick, 1991; Miller & Jackson, 1985.

7. The international authority on fear and anxiety, psychiatrist Isaac Marks (1987), makes this point well in discussing effective treatments for phobias. Exposure to the feared object is the central mechanism for change in fear. This was the principle the U. S. military employed in

changing attitudes toward racial integration in the armed services. At the time of this writing the U.S. military is once again employed in a similar debate on how to overcome prejudice against the prospective enlistment of homosexuals in the services. The intriguing question from a scientific point of view is how effective will exposure be for persons whose "prejudices" are the result of religious conviction, and whether prejudice has the same meaning here as it did for racial integration. On the other hand, we may recall that many people in the past used so-called "religious" justifications for segregation and denial of civil liberties to black Americans.

## 6. Reducing Obsessional Scruples

1. Marks, 1987.

2. Our nerve cells (neurons) have receptors which fit the molecules for the class of drugs known as benzodiazapenes (Valium, Librium, Halcion, etc.). Scientists believe that our bodies produce a natural benzodiazapene-like substance (ligand), since a similar discovery about opiate receptors led to the detection of naturally occurring opiate-like substances (endorphins).

3. Habituation comes from the Latin word *habitus* for condition or habit. The definition of habituation is to become accustomed to something by frequent repetition (*American Heritage Dictionary*, 1991, p. 596).

4. Barlow (1988) and Marks (1987) provide technical descriptions of habituation and exposure, as well as the theoretical controversies about how they might actually work to change nervous system responses. At this stage habituation is more a *description* of the change process than an explanation.

5. In behavioral terminology, the compulsion (e.g. checking, praying, washing, etc.) is *reinforcing* since it turns off the anxiety associated with the obsession.

6. Another term for blocking in the behavioral literature is response prevention.

7. One study of spouse involvement in the treatment of OCD found that patients who used partner-assisted exposure made more rapid improvement at the beginning (Emmelkamp & De Lange, 1983; see also Emmelkamp, de Haan, & Hoogduin, 1990).

8. A treatment study found that non-anxious but firm family members led to a more successful outcome than anxious or inconsistent members. If the family member argued or ridiculed, little improvement occurred (Mehta, 1990).

9. Greenberg & Witztum, 1991; Greenberg, Witztum, & Pisante, 1987.

10. Steketee & White, 1990.

11. Baer, 1992.

### 7. Reducing Compulsive Scruples

1. Linehan, 1993a, 1993b. She uses the term "mindfulness" to describe the desirable mental attitude for persons prone to self-injurious behaviors. The term itself echoes the work of social psychologist Ellen Langer (1989). I have reformulated the strategy under the rubric "reporter strategy" because I am mostly focusing on a single technique, rather than a new state of being. Also, Linehan's strategy evolved out of clinical work with women, and I have encountered some resistance to the term mindfulness from men. They seem more accepting of the phrase "reporter strategy." Readers familiar with Gestalt theory will recognize the similarity between this and what Perls calls "awareness training."

2. Mental health specialists in faith communities are reaching consensus that an immense paradox exists in the profile of religious individuals who engage in sexual misconduct (e.g. Ferder, 1986). Pedophiles, for example, most often fit the profile of a religiously and politically conservative individual, rather than the stereotype of a sexual libertarian (Ciarrocchi, 1993; Tollison & Adams, 1979). Specialists believe that the person more likely to act out is the individual who panics over the impulses and tries to suppress them with ferocious works of self-denial. This triggers the "white bear" phenomenon, which eventually wears down a person's defenses. Or, alternatively, excessive alcohol use may

disinhibit the remaining defenses. Readers need to recall that people with OCD do not act out their obsessional impulses.

Ideally, controlled research could determine if the reporter strategy lessens the frequency, intensity and duration of obsessions for a wide range of problems from OCD to sexual deviation. Presently we only have evidence of its effectiveness from clinical anecdotes.

3. Marks, 1987.

4. Royce, 1981.

## 8. Getting Help for Scruples and OCD

1. Pastoral counseling, however, has been defined with some degree of consensus (e.g. Estadt, Blanchette, & Comptom, 1991), but the *title* remains unregulated.

2. Christensen *et al.*, 1987; Cottraux *et al.*, 1990; Goodman *et al.*, 1990; Jenike, 1990; Jenike *et al.*, 1989; Kasvikis & Marks, 1988a, 1988b; Marks *et al.*, 1988; Mavissakalian & Jones, 1989; Mavissakalian, Jones, & Olson, 1990; Mavissakalian *et al.*, 1990; Montgomery, Montgomery & Fineberg, 1990; Pigott *et al.*, 1990; Thoren *et al.*, 1980.

3. Marks, 1987.

4. Fallon *et al.*, in press.

## 9. Technical Asides: Moral Reasoning, Scruples, and the Psychology of Religion

1. O'Flaherty, 1966, p.11.

2. This maxim, as we saw in Chapter 4, derives from a long moral theology tradition. In the Roman Catholic tradition, moral theology has lost its systematic emphasis since the Second Vatican Council (1962-65). Most discussions of conscience in contemporary moral theology are geared toward the topic of dissent—that is, when is it legitimate to follow one's own conscience in opposition to formal institutional teaching? Even a contemporary moral theology text which strongly maintains a traditional approach and has the full approval of church

hierarchy does not list scruples or scrupulosity in its index (Grisez, 1983). This may be a "sign of the times" that, given religion's struggle to maintain absolute moral standards, the issue of scruples captures little attention.

3. Jonsen & Toulmin, 1988. Their account resulted from experiences related to their work on a national panel of interdisciplinary experts attempting to solve ethical dilemmas in bio-medical research. They were impressed that experts from diverse philosophical traditions developed consensus when it came to practical ethical decisions, even though each person had completely different theoretical *explanations* for his or her opinion.

4. Church tradition has used the example of one of the great Fathers of the Church, Origen, to illustrate its disfavor with these literal interpretations. According to tradition, Origen was bothered by sexual temptations and castrated himself based on his literal interpretation of the cited texts. This act, reportedly, contributed to the church not recognizing him officially as a saint. The church does not want to encourage its members to engage in self-mutilation as a means of handling temptation. One could consider scrupulosity as a form of psychological self-mutilation.

5. Rapoport, 1990.

6. Here again, scrupulosity appears to resemble theoretical positions in classical moral theology. In the history of moral theology the position that one should act only if one chooses the morally strictest course was known as *tutiorism* (from the Latin word for safer) or rigorism. Roman Catholic Church authority condemned this position in 1690 (Grisez, 1983). The condemnation of this position again reinforces scrupulosity as an emotional disorder, not a disorder of conscience. People with scruples are not "tutiorists" in all matters, just in the select situations which trigger obsessions and compulsions. Sometimes, in an effort to motivate Catholic clients, I will point out the irony to them that, despite their extreme concern for orthodoxy, they are maintaining a condemned position. This requires careful clinical judgment and timing, because they may perceive this as one more torment.

7. Plath, 1971.

8. In the past, theologians have identified the two types I call developmental and clinical. C. Harney's article in the *New Catholic Encyclopedia* (1967) on "Scrupulosity" clearly delineates this tradition. The version I call milieu-influenced is also included in this tradition in seminal form. Tradition describes this version as due to faulty instruction. I have broadened the concept of instruction to take into account a wider array of environmental influences.

9. Tesson, 1964.

10. Developmental scrupulosity often responds to either external guidance and/or self-reflection. The historical examples cited (Luther, Bunyan, Ignatius) all found solutions in religious sources. As O'Flaherty notes (1966), however, it was not a mere intellectual conviction; each cure involved a "conscious *emotional* experience."

11. Bandura, 1986.

12. Fitz, 1990.

13. Masters & Johnson, 1970. An example of the positive influence of religion on sexual satisfaction in marriage can be seen in Rev. Andrew Greeley's *Faithful Attraction* (1991). This study found that a couple's praying together was strongly related to giving their sexual relationship high marks.

14. Kozak, Foa, & Steketee, 1988.

15. We cannot logically exclude alternative explanations—e.g. that people who develop such fears have rigid personality/cognitive structures that incorporate the religious messages in a selective, fear-arousing manner. This explanation sees the source of the fear within the dynamics of the listener rather than in the delivery of the message. Or, perhaps, like most psychological phenomena, an explanation requiring the interaction of both forces is most likely.

16. E.g. Cottraux *et al.*, 1990.

17. Religious groups that are in the midst of rapid sociological change represent a pronounced difficulty for scrupulous (and non-scrupulous)

members. The current state of the debate about dissent from official teaching in the Catholic Church is a good example. Since the end of the Second Vatican Council and with the public dissent of theologians and national bishops' conferences to the church's teaching on birth control, an atmosphere of sociological confusion regarding moral teaching exists. Although official teaching remains of one voice, the lived experience of the average Catholic is another matter. He or she is unlikely to hear much preaching from the pulpit on matters related to artificial birth control, and unlikely to see sexual topics treated in religious education that once received much attention (e.g. masturbation). My scrupulous clients experience this state of affairs as a form of "exposure" thrust upon them by their environment. That is, they have driving doubts and questions, but, unlike former days, will obtain little in the way of consensus from religious ministers servicing their local congregation. Whether this milieu fosters or reduces the potential development of scruples is an interesting question that awaits empirical research. Those interested in exploring the extreme alternative positions on moral authority in the church today might read Grisez (1983) which defends official teaching, or Curran & McCormick (1982) for a position that views dissent as beneficial to the church.

18. Greenberg, 1984.

19. Greenberg & Witztum, 1992.

20. Barlow, 1988.

21. O'Flaherty, 1973.

22. Estadt, Blanchette, & Compton, 1991; Wicks & Parsons, 1993.

23. One psychology teacher told our class that when he was a graduate student at the University of Indiana, Skinner paid a visit. Hearing that this student had potential for the field from the faculty, Skinner invited him to go for a walk. During the walk my teacher revealed that he was Catholic. This prompted Skinner to query as to how it was possible for a person to be *both* a psychologist and a Catholic!

24. Bergin, 1991.

25. E.g. Bandura, 1986. Behavioral and cognitive-behavioral approaches have not been totally neglected by those interested in the integration of psychology and religion. Those who have attempted straightforward integrations include Bufford, 1981; Miller & Jackson, 1985; Miller & Martin, 1988. Also, cognitive-behavioral approaches have a certain resemblance to many aspects of rational-emotive theory, and many theoretical and applied uses of RET exist in religious literature (e.g. Powell, 1969).

26. I am not advocating here a mindless smorgasbord approach to counselor training. Eclectic approaches are more difficult precisely because they require a personal integration within the context of a wealth of supervised experience. My comments are directed toward persons with advanced training.

27. Tesson, 1964, p.106.

28. Foa *et al.*, 1983.

29. Among varieties of pathological religious behavior we need to distinguish obsessional behavior from delusional behavior. Many authors believe these categories are more continuous than dichotomous in the religious sphere. This further complicates assessment and treatment. Hoffnung, Atzenberg, Hermesh & Munitz (1989) identify several criteria to distinguish obsessional religious beliefs from delusional or overvalued ideas. Persons with overvalued ideas tend to: 1) not seek help on their own but on the advice of others; 2) resist cooperating with behavioral strategies; 3) resist advice from a rabbi or clergyperson; 4) resist accepting medication; and 5) are inconsistent in their conformity to religious values— i.e. scrupulous in one area but indifferent or unobservant in others.

30. Propst *et al.*, 1992.

31. Jenike *et al.*, 1989.

# References

Akhatar, S., Wig, N. N., Varma, V. K., Pershad, D., & Verma, S. K. (1975). A phenomenological analysis of symptoms in obsessive-compulsive neurosis. *British Journal of Psychiatry, 127,* 342-348.

*American Heritage Dictionary: 2nd college edition.* (1991). Boston: Houghton Mifflin Co.

American Psychiatric Association (1987). *Diagnostic and statistical manual of mental disorders* (3rd ed. rev.). Washington, DC: Author.

Arterburn, S., & Felton, J. (1991). *Toxic faith: Understanding and overcoming religious addiction.* New York: Thomas Nelson, Publishers.

Baer, L. (1992). *Getting control: Overcoming your obsessions and compulsions.* New York: Penguin.

Bainton, T. (1950). *Here I stand.* New York: Abingdon Press.

Bandura, A. (1986). *Social foundations of thought and action.* Englewood Cliffs, NJ: Prentice-Hall.

Barlow, D. (1988). *Anxiety and its disorders: The nature and treatment of anxiety and panic.* New York: Guilford Press.

Bate, W. J. (1978). *Samuel Johnson.* London: Chatto & Windus.

Beck, A. T., Ward, C. M., Mendelson, M., Mach, J., & Erbaugh, J. (1961). An inventory for measuring depression. *Archives of General Psychiatry, 4,* 561-571.

Bergin, A. E. (1991). Values and religious issues in psychotherapy and mental health. *American Psychologist, 46,* 394-403.

Bickel, C. (1993). *Perceived stress, religious coping styles, and depressive affect.* Doctoral dissertation, Loyola College in Maryland.

Booth, L. (1992). *When God becomes a drug: Breaking the chains of religious addiction and abuse.* New York: Jeremy P. Tarcher, Inc.

Borkovec, T. D., Robinson, E., Pruzinsky, T., & DePress, J. A. (1983). Preliminary exploration of worry: Some characteristics and processes. *Behaviour Research and Therapy, 21,* 9-16.

Boswell, J. (1968). *The life of Samuel Johnson.* New York: Random House.

Brehm, J. W. (1966). *A theory of psychological reactance.* New York: Academic Press.

Bufford, R. K. (1981). *The human reflex.* New York: Harper & Row.

Bunyan, J. (1988). *Grace abounding: To the chief of sinners.* Westfield, NJ: Christian Library.

Caraman, P. (1990). *Ignatius Loyola: A biography of the founder of the Jesuits.* San Francisco: Harper & Row.

Carroll, M. G. (Ed.). (1964). *The treatment of scruples.* Techny, IL: Divine Word Publications.

Casey, D. (1948). *The nature and treatment of scruples: A guide for directors of souls.* Westminster, MD: Newman Press.

Christensen, H., Hadzi-Pavlovic, D., Andrews, G., & Mattick, R. (1987). Behavior therapy and tricyclic medication in the treatment of obsessive-compulsive disorder: A quantitative review. *Journal of Consulting and Clinical Psychology, 55,* 701-711.

Ciarrocchi, J. W. (1993). *A minister's handbook of mental disorders.* New York: Paulist Press.

Cottraux, J., Mollard, E., Bouvard, M., & Marks, I. (1990). A controlled study of fluvoxamine and exposure in obsessive-compulsive disorder. *International Clinical Psychopharmacology, 5,* 17-30.

Craighead, W. E., Kazdin, A. E., & Mahoney, M. J. (1976). *Behavior Modification: Principles, issues, and applications.* Boston: Houghton-Mifflin and Co..

Craske, M. G., Rapee, R. M., Jackel, L., & Barlow, D. H. (1989). Qualitative dimensions of worry in DSM-III-R generalized anxiety disorder subjects and nonanxious controls. *Behaviour Research and Therapy, 27,* 397-402.

Curran, C. E., & McCormick, R. A. (Eds.). (1982). *Readings in moral theology: No. 3: The magisterium and morality.* New York: Paulist Press.

Edwards, S., & Dickerson, M. (1987). Intrusive unwanted thoughts: A two-stage model of control. *British Journal of Medical Psychology, 60,* 317-328.

Emmelkamp, P. M., de Haan, E., & Hoogduin, C. A. (1990). Marital adjustment and obsessive-compulsive disorder. *British Journal of Psychiatry, 156*, 55-60.

Emmelkamp, P. M. G., & De Lange, I. (1983). Spouse involvement in the treatment of obsessive-compulsive patients. *Behaviour Research and Therapy, 21*, 341-346.

England, S. L., & Dickerson, M. (1988). Intrusive thoughts; unpleasantness and the major cause of uncontrollability. *Behaviour Research and Therapy, 26*, 279-282.

Estadt, B. K., Blanchette, M., & Compton, J. R. (1991). *Pastoral counseling* (rev. ed.). Englewood Cliffs, NJ: Prentice-Hall.

Fallon, B. A., Liebowitz, M. R., Hollander, E., Schneier, F., Campeas, R., Fairbanks, J., Papp, L., Hatterer, J., & Sandberg, D. The Pharmacotherapy of moral or religious scrupulosity. *Journal of Clinical Psychiatry*, in press.

Ferder, F. (1986). *Words made flesh*. Notre Dame, IN: Ave Maria Press.

Fitz, A. (1990). Religious and familial factors in the etiology of obsessive-compulsive disorder: A review. *Journal of Psychology and Theology, 18*, 141-147.

Fleming, L. (1978). *The Spiritual Exercises of St. Ignatius: A literal translation and a contemporary reading*. St. Louis: Institute of Jesuit Sources.

Foa, E. B., Grayson, J. B., Steketee, G. S., Doppelt, H. G., Turner, R. M., & Latimer, P. R. (1983). Success and failure in the behavioral treatment of obsessive-compulsives. *Journal of Consulting and Clinical Psychology, 51*, 287-297.

Foa, E. B., & Kozak, M. J. (1991). Diagnostic criteria for obsessive-compulsive disorder. *Hospital and Community Psychiatry, 42*, 679-680, 684.

Freund, B., & Steketee, G. (1989). Sexual history, attitudes and functioning of obsessive-compulsive patients. *Journal of Sex and Marital Therapy, 15*, 31-41.

Frost, R. O., Lahart, C. M., Dugas, K. M., & Sher, K. J. (1988). Information processing among non-clinical compulsives. *Behaviour Research and Therapy, 26*, 275-277.

Frost, R. O., & Sher, K. J. (1989). Checking behavior in a threatening situation. *Behaviour Research and Therapy, 27*, 385-389.

Frost, R. O., Sher, K. J., & Geen, T. (1986). Psychopathology and personality characteristics of nonclinical compulsive checkers. *Behaviour Research and Therapy*, *24*, 133-143.

Ganss, G. E. (1992). *The Spiritual Exercises of Saint Ignatius: A translation and commentary*. St. Louis: Institute of Jesuit Sources.

Goodman, W. K., Price, L. H., Delgado, P. L., & Palumbo, J. (1990). Specificity of serotonin reuptake inhibitors in the treatment of obsessive-compulsive disorder: Comparison of fluvoxamine and desipramine. *Archives of General Psychiatry*, *47*, 577-585.

Greeley, A. M. (1991). *Faithful attraction*. New York: Tom Doherty Associates.

Greenberg, D. (1984). Are religious compulsions religious or compulsive? *American Journal of Psychotherapy*, *38*, 524-532.

Greenberg, D., Witztum, E., & Pisante, J. (1987). Scrupulosity: Religious attitudes and clinical presentation. *British Journal of Medical Psychology*, *60*, 29-37.

Greenberg, D., & Witztum, E. (1991). The treatment of obsessive-compulsive disorder in strictly religious patients. In M. T. Pato & J. Zohar (Eds.), *Current treatments of obsessive-compulsive disorder* (pp. 157-172). Washington: American Psychiatric Press.

Greenberg, D., & Witztum, E. (1992). Content and prevalence of psychopathology in world religions. In J. F. Schumaker (Ed.), *Religion and mental health* (pp. 300-314). New York: Oxford University Press.

Grisez, G. (1983). *Christian moral principles*. Vol. 1. Chicago: Franciscan Herald Press.

Harney, C. (1967). Scrupulosity. In J. P. Whalen (Ed.), *New Catholic Encyclopedia* (pp. 1253-1255). Washington, DC: Catholic University of America.

Hoffnung, R., Atzenberg, D., Hermesh, H., & Munitz, H. (1989). Religious compulsions and the spectrum concept of psychopathology. *Psychopathology*, *22*, 141-144.

Honjo, S., Hirano, C., Murase, S., Kaneko, T., Sugiyama, T., Ohtaka, K., Aoyama, T., Takei, Y., Inoko, K., & Wakabayashi (1989). Obsessive-compulsive symptoms in childhood and adolescence. *Acta Psychiatrica Scandinavica*, *80*, 83-91.

Jenike, M. A. (1990). The pharmacological treatment of obsessive-compulsive disorders. *International Review of Psychiatry*, *2*, 411-425.

Jenike, M. A., Baer, L., Summergrad, P., Weilburg, J. B., Holland, A.,

& Seymour, R. (1989). Obsessive-compulsive disorder: A double-blind, placebo-controlled trial of clomipramine in 27 patients. *American Journal of Psychiatry, 146,* 1328-1330.

Jone, H., & Adelman, U. (1959). *Moral theology.* Westminster, MD: Newman Press.

Jonsen, A. R., & Toulmin, S. (1988). *The abuse of casuistry: A history of moral reasoning.* Berkeley: University of California Press.

Karno, M., Golding, J. M., Sorenson, S. B., & Audrey Burnam, M. (1988). The epidemiology of obsessive-compulsive disorder in five US communities. *Archives of General Psychiatry, 45,* 1094-1099.

Kasvikis, V., & Marks, I. M. (1988a). Clomipramine in obsessive-compulsive ritualisers treated with exposure therapy: Relations between dose, plasma levels, outcome and side effects. *Psychopharmacology, 95,* 113-118.

Kasvikis, Y., & Marks, I. (1988b). Clomipramine, self-exposure, and therapist-accompanied exposure in obsessive-compulsive ritualizers: Two-year follow-up. *Journal of Anxiety Disorders, 2,* 291-298.

Khanna, S., & Channabasavanna, S. M. (1988). Phenomenology of obsessions in obsessive-compulsive neurosis. *Psychopathology, 21,* 12-18

Kim, S. W., Dysken, M. W., & Katz, R. (1989). Rating scales for obsessive compulsive disorder. *Psychiatric Annals, 19,* 74-79.

Kim, S. W., Dysken, M. W. & Kuskowski, M. (1991). The Yale-Brown Obsessive-Compulsive Scale: A reliability and validity study. *Psychiatry Research, 34,* 99-106.

Kozak, M. J., Foa, E. B., & Steketee, G. (1988). Process and outcome of exposure treatment with obsessive-compulsives: Psychophysiological indicators of emotional processing. *Behavior Therapy, 19,* 157-169.

Kurtz, E. (1979). *Not-God: A history of Alcoholics Anonymous.* Center City, MN: Hazelden Press.

Langer, E. (1989). *Mindfulness.* New York: Addison-Wesley.

Larere, C. (1964). Pastoral behaviour towards the scrupulous. In M. G. Carroll (Ed.), *The treatment of scruples* (pp. 107-125). Techny, IL: Divine Word Publications.

Last, C. G., & Strauss, C. C. (1989). Obsessive-compulsive disorder in childhood. *Journal of Anxiety Disorders, 3,* 295-302.

Lauras, A. (1964). The scrupulous and the obsessed: A psychiatric study. In M. G. Carroll (Ed.), *The treatment of scruples* (pp. 11-87). Techny, IL: Divine Word Publications.

Linehan, M. M. (1993a). *Cognitive-behavioral treatment of borderline personality disorder*. New York: Guilford Press.

Linehan, M. M. (1993b). *Skills training manual for treating borderline personality disorders*. New York: Guilford Press.

Luxenberg, J. S., Swedo, S. E., Flament, M. F., & Friedland, R. P. (1988). Neuroanatomical abnormalities in obsessive-compulsive disorder detected with quantitative x-ray computed tomography. *American Journal of Psychiatry, 145*, 1089-1093.

Margulin, R. (1984). *Howard Hughes: His achievements and legacy*. Long Beach, CA: Wrather Port Properties.

Marks, I. M. (1978). *Living with fear*. New York: McGraw-Hill.

Marks, I. (1987). *Fears, Phobias, and Rituals: Panic, anxiety and their disorders*. New York: Oxford University Press.

Marks, I. M., Lelliott, P., Basoglu, M., Noshirvani, H., Monteiro, W., Cohen, D., & Kasvikis, Y. (1988). Clomipramine, self-exposure and therapist-aided exposure for obsessive-compulsive rituals. *British Journal of Psychiatry, 152*, 522-534.

Martinot, J. L., Mazoyer, B. M., Hanatouche, R., Huret, J. D., Legaut-Demare, F., Deslauriers, A. G., Hardyh, P., Pappata, S., Baron, J. C., & Syrota, A. (1990). Obsessive-compulsive disorder: A clinical, neuropsychological and positron emission tomography study. *Acta Psychiatrica Scandinavica, 82*, 233-242.

Masters, W. H., & Johnson, V. E. (1970). *Human sexual inadequacy*. Boston: Little, Brown.

Mavissakalian, M. R. (1979). Functional classification of obsessive-compulsive phenomena. *Journal of Behavioral Assessment, 1*, 271-279.

Mavissakalian, M., Hamann, M. S., & Jones, B. (1990a). DSM-III personality disorders in obsessive-compulsive disorders: Changes with treatment. *Comprehensive Psychiatry, 31*, 432- 437.

Mavissakalian, M., Hamann, M. S., & Jones, B. (1990b). Correlates of DSM-III personality disorder in obsessive-compulsive disorder. *Comprehensive Psychiatry, 31*, 481-489.

Mavissakalian, M. R., & Jones, B. A. (1989). Antidepressant drugs plus exposure treatment of agoraphobia/panic and obsessive-compulsive disorders. *International Review of Psychiatry, 1*, 275-281.

Mavissakalian, M. R., Jones, B. A., & Olson, S. C. (1990). Absence of placebo response in obsessive-compulsive disorder. *Journal of Nervous and Mental Disease, 178,* 268-270.

Mavissakalian, M. R., Jones, B., Olson, S., & Perel, J. M. (1990). Clomipramine in obsessive-compulsive disorder: Clinical response and plasma levels. *Journal of Clinical Psychopharmacology, 10,* 261-268.

McKeon, P., & Murray, R. (1987). Familial aspects of obsessive-compulsive neurosis. *British Journal of Psychiatry, 151,* 528-534.

Mehta, M. (1990). A comparative study of family-based and patient-based behavioural management in obsessive-compulsive disorder. *British Journal of Psychiatry, 157,* 133-135.

Meichenbaum, D., & Turk, D. C. (1987). *Facilitating treatment adherence.* New York: Plenum Press.

Meissner, W. W. (1992). *Ignatius of Loyola: The psychology of a saint.* New Haven: Yale University Press.

Miller, W. R. (1979). Behavioral treatment of problem drinkers: A comparative outcome study of three controlled drinking therapies. *Journal of Consulting and Clinical Psychology, 46,* 74-86.

Miller, W. R., & Jackson, K. A. (1985). *Practical psychology for pastors.* Englewood Cliffs, NJ: Prentice-Hall.

Miller, W. R., & Martin, J. E. (Eds.). (1988). *Behavior Therapy and Religion.* Beverly Hills: Sage Publications.

Miller, W. R., & Munoz, R. F. (1976). *How to control your drinking.* Englewood Cliffs, NJ: Prentice-Hall.

Miller, W. R., & Rollnick, S. (Eds.). (1991). *Motivational interviewing: Preparing people to change addictive behavior.* New York: Guilford Press.

Minichiello, W. E., Baer, L., Jenike, M. A., & Holland, A. (1990). Age of onset of major subtypes of obsessive-compulsive disorder. *Journal of Anxiety Disorders, 4,* 147-150.

Modell, J. G., Mountz, J. M., Curtis, G. C., & Greden, J. F. (1989). Neurophysiologic dysfunction in basal ganglia/limbic striatal and thalamocortical circuits as a pathogenetic mechanism of obsessive-compulsive disorder. *Journal of Neuropsychiatry, 1,* 27-36.

Montgomery, S. A., Montgomery, D. B., & Fineberg, N. (1990). Early response with clomipramine in obsessive compulsive disorder— A placebo controlled study. *Neuro-Psychopharmacology and Biological Psychiatry, 14,* 719-727.

Murphy, D. L., & Pigott, T. A. (1990). A comparative examination of a role for serotonin in obsessive compulsive disorder, panic disorder, and anxiety. *Journal of Clinical Psychiatry, 51* (Supplement), 53-58.

Myers, J. K., Weissman, M. M., Tischler, G. L., Holzer, C. E., Leaf, P.J., Orvaschel, H. A., Anthony, J. C., Boyd, J. H., Burke, J. E., Kramer, M., & Stolzmann, R. (1984). Six-month prevalence of psychiatric disorders in three communities: 1980-1982. *Archives of General Psychiatry, 41*, 959-967.

Neale, J. M., & Liebert, R. M. (1986). *Science and behavior: An introduction to methods of research.* Englewood Cliffs, NJ: Prentice-Hall.

*The New American Bible* (1988). Mission Hills, CA: Benziger Publishing Co.

Niler, E. R., & Beck, S. J. (1989). The relationship among guilt, dysphoria, anxiety and obsessions in a normal population. *Behaviour Research and Therapy, 27*, 213-220.

O'Flaherty, V. M. (1966). *How to cure scruples.* Milwaukee: Bruce Publishing Co..

O'Flaherty, V. M. (1973). Therapy for scrupulosity. In R-R. M. Jurjevich (Ed.), *Direct psychotherapy: 28 American originals* (pp. 221-243). Coral Gables, FL: University of Miami Press.

Paul VI, Pope. (1968). *On the regulation of birth: Humanae vitae, encyclical letter.* Washington, DC: United States Catholic Conference.

Peele, S. (1989). *Diseasing of America: Addiction treatment out of control.* Lexington, MA: Lexington Books.

Pfohl, B., Black, D., Noyes, R., Kelley, M., & Blum, N. (1990). A test of the tridimensional personality theory: Association with diagnosis and platelet imipramine binding in obsessive-compulsive disorder. *Biological Psychiatry, 28*, 41-46.

Pigott, T. A., Pato, M. T., Bernstein, S. E., Grover, G. N., Hill, J. L., Tolliver, T. J., & Murphy, D. L. (1990). Controlled comparisons of clomipramine and fluoxetine in the treatment of obsessive-compulsive disorder. *Archives of General Psychiatry, 47*, 926-932.

Plath, S. (1971). *The bell jar.* New York: Harper and Row.

Pollak, J. (1987). Obsessive-compulsive personality: Theoretical and clinical perspective and recent research findings. *Journal of Personality Disorders, 1*, 248-262.

Powell, J. (1969). *Why am I afraid to tell you who I am?* Niles, IL: Argus.

Prochaska, J. O., & Di Clemente, C. C. (1986). Towards a comprehensive model of change. In W. R. Miller & N. Heather (Eds.), *Treating addictive behavior: Process of change* (pp. 3-27). New York: Plenum Press.

Propst, R. L., Ostrom, R., Watkins, P., Dean, T., & Mashburn, D. (1992). Comparative efficacy of religious and nonreligious cognitive-behavioral therapy for the treatment of clinical depression in religious individuals. *Journal of Consulting and Clinical Psychology, 60,* 94-103.

Puhl, L. H. (1951). *The Spiritual Exercises of St. Ignatius: Based on studies in the language of the autograph.* Chicago: Loyola University Press.

Rachman, S., & De Silva, P. (1978). Abnormal and normal obsessions. *Behaviour Research and Therapy, 16,* 233-248.

Rachman, S. (1976). The modification of obsessions: A new formulation. *Behaviour Research and Therapy, 14,* 437-443.

Rachman, S. J., & Hodgson, R. J. (1980). *Obsessions and compulsions.* Englewood Cliffs, NJ: Prentice-Hall.

Rapoport, J. L. (1990). *The boy who couldn't stop washing: The experience and treatment of obsessive-compulsive disorder.* New York: New American Library.

Rasmussen, S., & Eisen, J. (1990). Epidemiology and clinical features of obsessive-compulsive disorders. In M. A. Jenike, L. Baer, & W. E. Minichiello (Eds.), *Obsessive-compulsive disorders: Theory and management,* second edition. Chicago: Year Book Medical Publishers.

Rasmussen, S. A., & Tsuang, M. T. (1986). Clinical characteristics and family history in DSM-III obsessive-compulsive disorder. *American Journal of Psychiatry, 143,* 317-322.

Regier, D., Narrow, W. E., & Rae, D. S. (1990). The epidemiology of anxiety disorders: The Epidemiologic Catchement Area (ECA) experience. *Journal of Psychiatric Research, 24, Suppl. 2,* 3-14.

Royce, J. E. (1981). *Alcohol problems and alcoholism: A comprehensive survey.* New York: Free Press.

Salkoviskis, P. M. (1989). Cognitive-behavioural factors and the persistence of intrusive thoughts in obsessional problems. *Behaviour Research and Therapy, 27,* 677-682.

Salkoviskis, P. M. & Harrison, J. (1984). Abnormal and normal obsessions—a replication. *Behaviour Research and Therapy, 22,* 549-552.

Schumaker, J. (Ed.). (1992). *Religion and mental health.* New York: Oxford University Press.

Sher, K. J., Frost, R. O., Kushner, M., Crews, T. M., & Alexander, J. E. (1989). Memory deficits in compulsive checkers: Replication and extension in a clinical sample. *Behaviour Research and Therapy, 27,* 65-69.

Sher, K., Frost, R. O., & Otto, R. (1983). Cognitive deficits in compulsive checkers: An exploratory study. *Behaviour Research and Therapy, 21,* 357-363.

Sher, K. J., Mann, B., & Frost, R. O. (1984). Cognitive dysfunction in compulsive checkers: Further explorations. *Behaviour Research and Therapy, 5,* 493-502.

Sher, K. J., Martin, E. D., Raskin, G., & Perrigo, R. (1991). Prevalence of DSM-III-R disorders among nonclinical compulsive checkers and noncheckers in a college student sample. *Behaviour Research and Therapy, 29,* 479-483.

Simpson, D. P. (Ed.). (1960). *Cassell's new Latin dictionary.* New York: Funk & Wagnalls Co.

Skinner, B. F. (1972). *Beyond freedom and dignity.* New York: Bantam/Vantage Books.

Stanley, M. A., Turner, S. M., & Borden, J. W. (1990). Schizotypal features in the obsessive-compulsive disorder. *Comprehensive Psychiatry, 31,* 611-618.

Steketee, G. (1990). Personality traits and disorders in obsessive-compulsives. *Journal of Anxiety Disorders, 4,* 351-364.

Steketee, G., & Tynes, L. L. (1991). Behavioral treatment of obsessive-compulsive disorder and other anxiety disorders. In M. T. Pato & J. Zohar (Eds.), *Current treatments of obsessive-compulsive disorder* (pp. 61-86). Washington: American Psychiatric Press.

Steketee, G., & White, K. (1990). *When once is not enough: Help for obsessive compulsives.* Oakland, CA: New Harbinger Publications.

Steketee, G., Grayson, J., & Foa, E. B. (1987). A comparison of characteristics of obsessive-compulsive disorder and other anxiety disorders. *Journal of Anxiety Disorders, 1,* 325-335.

Steketee, G., Quay, S., & White, K. (1991). Religion and guilt in OCD patients. *Journal of Anxiety Disorders, 5*, 359-367.

Tesson, E. (1964). Doctrinal history. In M. G. Carroll (Ed.), *The treatment of scruples* (pp. 88-106). Techny, IL: Divine Word Publications.

Thoren, P., Asberg, M., Bertilsson, L., Meilstrom, B., Sjoqvist, F., & Traskman, L. (1980). Clomipramine treatment of obsessive-compulsive disorder: II. Biochemical aspects. *Archives of General Psychiatry, 37*, 1289-1295.

Toates, F. (1990). *Obsessional thoughts and behaviour: Help for obsessive-compulsive disorder*. Wellingborough, Northhamptonshire: Thorsons Publishers.

Tollison, C. D., & Adams, H. E. (1979). *Sexual disorders: Theory, treatment and research*. New York: Gardner.

Turner, S. M., Beidel, D. C., & Nathan, R. S. (1985). Biological factors in obsessive-compulsive disorders. *Psychological Bulletin, 97*, 430-450.

Turner, S. M., Beidel, D. C., & Stanley, M. A. (1992). Are obsessional thoughts and worry different cognitive phenomena? *Clinical Psychology Review, 12*, 257-270.

Warwick, H. M. C., & Salkoviskis, P. M. (1990). Unwanted erections in obsessive-compulsive disorder. *British Journal of Psychiatry, 157*, 919-921.

Wegner, D. (1989). *White bears and other unwanted thoughts: Suppression, obsession, and the psychology of mental control*. New York: Viking.

Whitaker, A., Johnson, J., Shaffer, D., Rapoport, J. L., Kalikow, K., Walsh, B. T., Davies, M., Braiman, S., & Dolinsky, A. (1990). Uncommon troubles in young people: Prevalence estimates of selected psychiatric disorders in a nonreferred population. *Archives of General Psychiatry, 47*, 487-496.

Wicks, R. J., & Parsons, R. D. (Eds.). (1993). *Clinical handbook of pastoral counseling*, Vol. 2. New York: Paulist Press.

Wicks, R. J., Parsons, R. D., & Capps, D. (Eds.). (1993). *Clinical handbook of pastoral counseling*, Vol. 1 (expanded ed). New York: Paulist Press.

Zitterl, W., Lenz, G., Mairhofer, A., & Zapotoczky, H. G. (1990). Obsessive-compulsive disorder: Course and interaction with depression. *Psychopathology, 23*, 73-80.

# Index

Agnostic 98-99, 128
Alcoholics Anonymous 66
Alcoholism 26-27
Alprazolam 108
American Association of Pastoral
    Counselors (AAPC) 107
American Psychological
    Association 111
Anafranil 30, 107
*Anxiety and Its Disorders* 112
Anxiety Disorders Association of
    America 109
Aquinas, Thomas 92
Aristotle 114, 116
Ativan 108
Augustine, Saint 34

Baer, Lee 110
Barlow, David 25, 26, 30, 112
Behavior therapy 13-14, 30, 50,
    108-109
*Bell Jar, The* 120
Benzodiazapenes 109
Bergin, Allen 13
Biological treatment 29-30, 31
Blasphemy 36, 57
Blocking (see also Response
    Prevention) 76-77, 87-93
*Boy Who Couldn't Stop Washing,*
    *The* 104, 111

Bunyan, John 11, 32-40, 41, 89

Casuistry 115
Catholic Church 48, 109
Cicero 116
Clomipramine 30, 107
Compulsions
    changing 87
    checking 22-23
    confessing 23
    counting 23
    definition 17, 56
    hoarding 24
    symmetry 23
    washing 23
Counselor, licensed/
    certified 106

Depression 27, 38
Descartes, Rene 114

Exposure 73-76, 77, 80-86

*Fears, Phobias, and Rituals* 112
Fluoxetine 30, 107
Foa, Edna 105, 126
Freud, Sigmund 51

*Getting Control* 110-111
*Grace Abounding* 32-40

179